D1560280

STRANGELY FAMILIAR

STRANGELY FAMILIAR:
DESIGN AND EVERYDAY LIFE

745.2
B613s

ANDREW BLAUVELT
WALKER ART CENTER, MINNEAPOLIS

OIL CITY LIBRARY
2 CENTRAL AVENUE
OIL CITY, PA. 16301

Published on the occasion of the exhibition *Strangely Familiar: Design and Everyday Life*, curated by Andrew Blauvelt for the Walker Art Center.

Walker Art Center
Minneapolis, Minnesota
June 8–September 7, 2003

Carnegie Museum of Art
Pittsburgh, Pennsylvania
November 8, 2003–February 15, 2004

Lille 2004 Capitale Européenne de la Culture
Musée de l'Hospice Comtesse
Lille, France
September 4–November 28, 2004

The North American tour of *Strangely Familiar: Design and Everyday Life* is made possible by generous support from Target Stores.

Additional funding for this exhibition is provided by the Mondriaan Foundation, with support from the Netherlands Culture Fund of the Dutch Ministries for Foreign Affairs and Education, Culture, and Science; and The Prince Bernhard Cultural Foundation. In-kind assistance provided by Bouwbedrijf De Nijs and Kirin Brewery Company, Ltd.

The exhibition catalogue is made possible in part by a grant from the Andrew W. Mellon Foundation in support of Walker Art Center publications.

Major support for Walker Art Center programs is provided by the Minnesota State Arts Board through an appropriation by the Minnesota State Legislature, the Lila Wallace-Reader's Digest Fund, The Bush Foundation, the Doris Duke Charitable Foundation through the Doris Duke Fund for Jazz and Dance and the Doris Duke Performing Arts Endowment Fund, Target Stores, Marshall Field's, and Mervyn's with support from the Target Foundation, The McKnight Foundation, General Mills Foundation, Coldwell Banker Burnet, the Institute of Museum and Library Services, the National Endowment for the Arts, American Express Philanthropic Program, The Regis Foundation, The Cargill Foundation, U.S. Bank, Star Tribune Foundation, 3M, and the members of the Walker Art Center.

CONTENTS

DESIGNERS

PROJECTS

As a distinctly human and self-conscious intervention, design distinguishes the civilized world from the natural realm. To design some place, some thing, or some message has been a basic capacity from the beginning of human consciousness; this expressive drive revolves around our collective and individual need to transform our physical environment in both decorative and profoundly functional ways. All aspects of our material world have been touched and, hence, designed in some way. This plethora of spaces, objects, and messages shapes, in both recognized and subversive ways, almost every aspect of our daily lives. Despite—perhaps even because of—its ubiquitous presence, design as both a noun and verb remains an elusive subject to the general public. This is but one reason that the Walker Art Center has a long-standing commitment both to promoting and practicing good design. For many years it has sheltered an award-winning in-house design department that produces all of the graphic materials—from books to monthly calendars to branding campaigns—by which this institution communicates with its diverse constituencies. In addition, the department invites two designers each year to participate in an internship program, thus helping train the practitioners who will lead the field in the future.

In fact, the Walker has been deeply involved in giving intellectual shape to the world of design for more than sixty years. In 1941, William Defenbacher, who was trained as an architect and became the Walker's first public director, established the reputation of this institution with a series of pioneering projects about modern design: The Idea Houses, full-scale modern homes built on the grounds of the Walker in the 1940s; The Everyday Art Gallery; and the publication *Everyday Art Quarterly* all championed the good design movement of the mid-20th century. These projects were among the first of their kind in the United States. During the 1970s and 1980s, the Walker organized many groundbreaking exhibitions under the creative oversight of Mildred Friedman, who also served as the director of the design department. These exhibitions include *Sottsass/Superstudio: Mindscapes* (1973), *The Architecture of Frank Gehry* (1986), *Graphic Design in America: A Visual Language History* (1989), and the series *Architecture Tomorrow* (1988–1991) with Frank Israel, Morphosis, Diller+Scofidio, Steven Holl, Stanley Saitowitz, and Tod Williams/Billie Tsien, who were all emerging architects at the time. That legacy of creating and exhibiting progressive design continued under the leadership of former design directors Laurie Haycock Makela and Matt Eller and is fortified by Andrew Blauvelt, the present director and curator of the exhibition that prompts these recollections. Projects from the 1990s to the present include commissions such as the development of Matthew Carter's innovative typeface Walker (1994–1995), and clearly the design of the art center's proposed expansion by Herzog & de Meuron, Basel, Switzerland, in cooperation with Hammel, Green, and Abrahamson, Inc., Minneapolis, also signals the Walker's desire to contribute to the cultural and civic landscape.

Blauvelt's insights into both the practical and speculative aspects of design have greatly benefited this institution; he is simultaneously a demanding teacher and a caring partner, pushing us all to better articulate what matters most and to whom we are speaking in order to develop design concepts that are clear, elegant, inventive, and reflective of the Walker's mission. *Strangely Familiar: Design and Everyday Life* brings together more than thirty projects by artists, architects, and designers from various parts of the world. These works illuminate myriad conditions of contemporary life, such as the nomadic way we construct our lives, create islands of artificial nature, respond to dynamic rather than mute objects that change their form and function, and wittingly participate in the design of those things that surround us. All of the projects, whether built, in production, or in the form of visionary proposals or concepts, afford an opportunity for us to question what we typically take for granted in the creation of the material world.

A project of this scope and complexity would not have been possible without the very generous contributions of those who share the Walker's commitment to fostering the very best of design and bring this enthusiasm and excitement to the public. We are deeply grateful for the unstinting support of Target Stores, which makes this exhibition and its North American tour possible. I am particularly grateful to Michael Francis, Senior Vice-President of Marketing for the Target Corporation and one of the most princely of Walker Board members, for his early delight in the possibilities this exhibition offered. Many of us trade nearly daily stories about our Target "finds," since the company has aligned itself with some of the most important designers working today. We would also like to express our gratitude to the Mondriaan Foundation with support from the Netherlands Culture Fund of the Dutch Ministries for Foreign Affairs and Education, Culture, and Science; and the Prince Bernhard Cultural Foundation, whose assistance makes possible the presentation of works from the Netherlands.

Kathy Halbreich, Director

ACKNOWLEDGMENTS

Strangely Familiar: Design and Everyday Life would not be possible without the participation and cooperation of many individuals who collectively helped realize the exhibition and its accompanying publication.

First and foremost, I extend my deepest gratitude to the more than fifty artists, architects, and designers who provided the creative energy necessary to realize the works we have assembled for this project.

I am indebted to the essayists—Jonathan Bell, Aaron Betsky, and Jamer Hunt—for their commentaries on the contemporary conditions of design. Their insights into the elusive but potent nature of design offer important intellectual contexts with which to better understand and engage the work.

The ability to assemble the diversity of projects shown would not have been possible without the generosity of those collections, galleries, and companies willing to share their works with a larger public. The names of all exhibition lenders can be found in the checklist on pages 331–342. I would like to acknowledge Valerie Imus and Leigh Markopoulos at the CCAC Wattis Institute for Contemporary Art, San Francisco, who helped us secure Shigeru Ban's *Paper Loghouse*; Sabina Rivetti at C.P. Company, who fulfilled our many requests; John and Jean Geresi, Houston, for their generous loan of Marcel Wanders' works; and Lucy M. Everett and Amanda Robinson at the Terrance Conran Collection, London.

Special thanks must go to Bonnie G. Kelm, director, and Christopher Scoates, chief curator, at the University Art Museum, University of California at Santa Barbara, for their development of the *MDU* project by LOT-EK and for their graciousness in allowing the Walker to debut this important new work.

This exhibition would not be feasible without the generous financial support of those organizations dedicated to bringing design to a wider audience. I am particularly indebted to Target Stores for their support of the North American tour, including its debut in Minneapolis. Important funding to present works from the Netherlands was provided by the Mondriaan Foundation with support from the Netherlands Culture Fund of the Dutch Ministries for Foreign Affairs and Education, Culture, and Science; and the Prince Bernhard Cultural Foundation. Lowry Hill Investments sponsored the preview dinner and *MPLS.ST.PAUL* Magazine provided promotional support. In-kind assistance was generously provided by De Nijs building company and Kirin Brewery Company, Ltd.

I would like to acknowledge our tour partners for bringing the exhibition to audiences in their communities: at the Carnegie Museum of Art, Richard Armstrong, director, Sarah Nichols, chief curator, and Ray Ryan and Tracy Myers, curators of architecture; and at Lille 2004, Didier Fusillier, director, Martine Aubry, president and mayor of Lille, and Caroline David, chief of visual arts.

At the Walker Art Center my gratitude goes to director Kathy Halbreich for her unwavering support of progressive design in all of its manifestations, and chief curator Richard Flood for providing invaluable assistance in the exhibition's planning and realization.

My colleagues in visual arts provided important advice on organizing the exhibition, including curator Philippe Vergne and associate curator Douglas Fogle, who skillfully helped me navigate the complexities of the exhibition's budgeting. Administrative assistant Lynn Dierks tackled the intricacies of the exhibition planning, and I thank her for her tenacity in developing the tour schedule. Most importantly, curatorial interns Alisa Eimen and Sara Marion provided crucial support, undertook extensive research, and generated great enthusiasm for the project over the course of its two-year gestation.

Registrar Elizabeth Peck expertly managed the handling of art and oversaw the complicated coordination of shipping from around the world. Cameron Zebrun and his staff in program services—in particular, David Dick, crew chief—attended to the myriad demands of installation with their usual expertise and professionalism.

Ann Bitter, administrative director, and Mary Polta, finance director, kept the project on solid financial footing. Christopher Stevens, development director, Kathryn Ross, director of special projects fund-raising, and especially Sarah Sargent, grant writer, were tireless in their efforts to make the exhibition a fiscal reality. I would like to thank Scott Winter, director of membership and visitor services, for his powers of late-night listening, and his staff, who arranged another wonderful late-night exhibition preview.

I would like to acknowledge the support of Sarah Schultz, director of education and community programs, and her staff. In particular, Meredith Walters, associate director of public programs, helped organize the opening-day activities; Kiyoko Motoyama Sims, associate director of community programs, arranged a place for the *MDU*; and Lara Roy, assistant director of tours and family programs, as well as the many tour and information guides, provided physical and interpretive access to the works.

Steve Dietz, curator of new media initiatives, handled the development of our collective telematic ambitions and supervised the design competition for what eventually became the *Dialog* project.

Finally, I extend deep gratitude to my staff in the design studio for indulging me in this effort. Kathleen McLean edited this publication with aplomb, and Pamela Johnson copyedited, lending her keen attention to detail. Lisa Middag, publications manager, supervised the catalogue's production and provided invaluable assistance, while David Naj, production artist, ensured the quality of the images. Alex DeArmond, graphic designer, worked tirelessly and collaboratively to produce such a beautiful book.

Andrew Blauvelt, Design Director

ANDREW BLAUVELT

STRANGELY FAMILIAR: DESIGN AND EVERYDAY LIFE

Design in the Age of Design

A paradoxical presence in our lives, design is both invisible and conspicuous, familiar and strange. It surrounds us while fading from view, becoming second nature and yet seemingly unknowable. Broadly conceived as
the world of human-made artifacts, design is everywhere: the tools we use,
the furnishings we keep, the clothes we wear, the cars we drive, the books
we read, the houses where we dwell, the offices where we work, and the
cities in which we live. Even nature does not escape the reach of design,
whether a park, a new species of plant, or the manipulation of human bodies and genes. In a typical day the average person encounters hundreds of
objects and thousands of messages, each designed by someone.

Despite this utter ubiquity, design remains for many people a mysterious force. This is in part because it presents itself through the myriad
objects and images it creates—autonomous and mute things, which tend
to conceal rather than reveal the process of their making. Thus, the vast
majority of people come into contact with design as consumers learning
to discern among innumerable offerings. Far fewer individuals have access
to designers or are privy to the processes employed by them. While the
activity of design is pervasive and the numbers of professionals who

engage in it are quite vast in any modern society, most design escapes notice, emerging from the landscape or entering the world rather quietly, often anonymously. The relative invisibility of design is also a matter of perceptual survival. Most new things are quickly absorbed into our immediate surroundings, forming the background against which we go about our everyday lives. Without this ability to integrate objects into our environment, the world would seem a daunting place — an ever-changing visual cacophony.

Just as design populates a familiar world, it can also stand apart from it. Modern societies demand designs that create distinctions by signaling what is different or new. During the 1990s there was a marked increase in design awareness within the media, among businesses, in the government, and most certainly in the culture at large. There are numerous markers for this conspicuousness: Frank Gehry's design of the Guggenheim Bilbao, which inaugurated the phenomenon of spectacle architecture; the introduction of numerous self-consciously designed products, such as Apple Computer's multicolored iMacs and Nike's proliferation of footwear styles; or Prime Minister Tony Blair's rebranding of British heritage as "Cool Britannia." No longer the province of specialty shops with inaccessible prices, mass-market retailers promoted the democratization of design at the international furnishings company IKEA, or in once unthinkable places such as the home of the "bluelight special," K-Mart, whose aisles now stock domestic denizen Martha Stewart's line of housewares. Other retailers such as Target produced signature collections by architect Michael Graves and designers such as Todd Oldham and Philippe Starck. Not content to fill only the pages of specialist journals, design became a subject for newspapers and mainstream magazines, and spawned new publishing genres. The concept of lifestyle coalesced; that elusive but identifiable thing united such disparate patterns as one's preferences in clothing, automobiles, and furniture with tastes in music, movies, travel, and cuisine and packaged it under titles such as *Wallpaper** or *Martha Stewart Living* (to name only two). Today design is expected to perform in an ensemble cast, no longer as a wallflower or mere product feature, but in a starring role in a story where branding, lifestyle, and products form various narratives of consumer experience.

15

1. B. Joseph Pine II
and James H.
Gilmore, "Welcome
to the Experience
Economy," in *Harvard
Business Review*
(July–August 1998):
97–105.

2. Product designer
Karim Rashid claims
to have coined the
term "blobjects." See
his essay "Blobism" in
*Karim Rashid: I Want
to Change the World*,
(New York: Universe,
2001). For a discus-
sion of "blobitecture,"
and other aspects of
digitally produced
architecture, see
Architecture 89, no. 9
(September 2000).

The aforementioned examples belie the invisibility of design in the world at large. Indeed, they map the terrain in which design emerged as a potent force transforming products into lifestyles, companies into brands, and neighborhoods into destinations. Design in the 1990s exemplified the transformation of the economy from its postindustrial condition (which was after all only a symptom) to its more synergistic guise—what economists James Gilmore and Joseph Pine have famously termed the "experience economy."[1] In such an economy, products are merely props in the staging of memorable moments of consumption. In economies of the past, we understood the function of goods in terms of exchange value (worth) or use value (utility). The experience economy represents the systematic development of what philosopher Jean Baudrillard refers to as sign value (meaning). Like a medieval cosmology where objects are imbued with mysterious meanings, nothing represents itself literally in the world of experience economies: sneakers are signs of wellness, competitiveness, and prestige, and coffee is no longer just a drink but the nexus of social conviviality and a barometer of lifestyle. This suggests that objects are merely nodes in a larger web of references and connections in which consumptive desires, patterns, and actions are central.

The design fields responded to the needs of this economy by producing a plethora of new things. The 1990s were the most prolific and important years for design since the 1960s. This vitality could be seen in the massive building boom that demanded more inventive and expressive forms of architecture, or in glitzy new consumer products—mobile phones, digital audio players, other handheld electronics, or even the more pedestrian garbage cans, toothbrushes, and staplers—whose forms were undergoing rapid change. With computer-aided design programs, contemporary culture has been visually transformed by the spline curve, adding sinuous edges to everything from buildings to cars to sneakers in what promoters and detractors have come to call "blobjects" and "blobitecture."[2] It is both tempting and plausible to view the last ten years as an exercise in this new styling, a contemporaneous version of 1930s streamlining. However, despite the increasingly seductive products on offer, it would be misleading to focus solely on this formal aspect of design.

A comparison of the last decade's output to the 1960s is instructive. In many ways, one sensed an air of optimism, even an unbridled enthusiasm, about the possibilities of design—the same attitude that pervaded the youthful exuberance surrounding inflatable furniture, modish environments, and geodesic housing of thirty years prior. In fact, many contemporary designers acknowledge their inspiration from sources such as the visionary architectural proposals of Archigram; the fluid, colorful spaces and mod furniture of Verner Panton; or the social consciousness espoused by design gurus Victor Papenak and Buckminster Fuller. The spirit of social liberation that spawned various possibilities for alternative living in the sixties (communes, bachelor pads, converted school buses, or even imagined colonies in outer space) has its contemporary corollary in the desire for evermore connected but mobile lifestyles and all of the things that go with it. The ecological imperative of the *Whole Earth Catalog* or Fuller's *Operating Manual for Spaceship Earth* finds its 1990s equivalent in "green architecture" with, for instance, its rooftop garden schemes, and in "disassembly lines," by which manufacturers can reclaim the components of their discarded products.

Certainly it would be possible to view many segments of recent design through these perspectives of formal evolution, historical zeitgeist, technological change, or ecological concern. Many books and exhibitions have done precisely that. Instead, the exhibition *Strangely Familiar: Design and Everyday Life* takes a broader approach, examining a range of projects across many areas of design. What connects these disparate works are a strong conceptual basis and a desire to rethink certain assumptions about design by offering us imaginative and often strange solutions. These projects force us to look at our everyday world anew, challenge our own presumptions about what is possible, and reconsider our relationship to things that once seemed so familiar.

If the last decade has been about the special nature of design—its strange and conspicuous presence in our world—then there has been a countervailing need to examine the more mundane and familiar world of daily life. The everyday is an elusive subject, a kind of residual realm encompassing those activities, practices, spaces, and things that exist beyond or beside the reach of society's official dictates and actions. It can be said that the everyday acts as a foil to design's increasingly active presence in the world. Conversely, design can be the measure by which we gauge our encounter with the everyday.

3. Georges Perec, "Approaches to What?", in *Species of Spaces and Other Pieces*, ed. John Sturrock (London: Penguin Books, 1997), 210.

Thinking about the Everyday

"How should we take account of, question, describe what happens every day and recurs every day: the banal, the quotidian, the obvious, the common, the ordinary, the infraordinary, the background noise, the habitual?"
– Georges Perec[3]

The quotidian has long been a touchstone for many artists and movements, from scenes of daily life famously detailed in seventeenth-century Dutch paintings or the once-shocking ordinariness of Postimpressionist subject matter. No longer content with depicting daily life, artists soon sought to disrupt it. Duchamp's "readymades" and the Surrealists' oneiric tableaux transformed mundane objects, radically altering their once familiar contexts. As modern artists sought to join art with life, everyday practices became a principle component of their work, from the gamelike strategies of Fluxus to the Situationists' technique of the *dérive* (partially programmed wanderings through the city), to the unflinching recording of banal activities in the Andy Warhol films *Sleep* or *Eat*. In both artistic practice and intellectual inquiry, the everyday as a subject of critical examination developed in the postwar period with the advent of a modern consumer society. In the social sciences, the quotidian has been studied for decades by philosophers such as Henri Lefebvre and Michel de Certeau or writers like Georges Perec. Each of these individuals provides a departure point for understanding the role of everyday life.

Lefebvre, in his pioneering analysis first published in 1947, *Critique de la vie quotidienne* (*The Critique of Everyday Life*), argues that the quotidian as the subject of philosophical study had been long neglected, treated as trivial in favor of "higher" or more serious topics. Because everyday life was particular and concrete and had to be lived to be truly understood, he faulted the abstract, systematic theories of then-evolving studies such as structural anthropology and semiotics. Born at the turn of the twentieth century, Lefebvre saw French daily life eroded by the effects of modernization. By suggesting the alienation experienced in modern society, which estranged people from a once holistic conception of life and work through the fragmentation and specialization of industrialized labor, Lefebvre argues against what much of everyday life had been reduced to, namely the drudgery and repetitiveness of work, bureaucratic social control, and empty consumerism. It is difficult to locate in his writings any direction for design to take, because in so many ways it contributes to the very problems he identifies: the mechanisms of advertising to create desire, the proliferation of identical consumer goods, and the rationalized strictures of modern urban planning. Nevertheless, his 1974 treatise *La production de l'espace* (*The Production of Space*) has influenced recent thinking in the fields of urbanism and architecture (undoubtedly due in part to its translation into English in 1991). As the title indicates, Lefebvre understands space as neither natural nor abstract, but rather as something that is consciously created, and in turn, produces specific effects. He countered the idea of classical and modernist notions of a universal, abstract space dominated by the visual by proposing instead a social space composed of differences. For him, space is a social product, not a neutral container, one that can encourage or discourage certain practices and behaviors.

Perhaps not surprisingly, his ideas about the ideological nature of space were of interest to those involved in architecture and urban planning during the 1980s and 1990s, a time when such subjects were increasingly examined, no matter how belatedly, through the lenses of gender, race, and class. This also signals a shift away from the modernist preoccupation with formal aspects to a more postmodernist stance considering content or effect. Contained within *The Production of Space* is a fictitious exchange in which Lefebvre answers his critics who would complain that true creativity lies within formal innovation itself. One side contends that "for architects who concern themselves primarily with content, as for 'users,' as for the activity of dwelling itself—all these merely reproduce outdated forms. They are in no sense innovative forces."[4] Lefebvre replies: "Surely there comes a moment when formalism is exhausted, when only a new injection of con-

4. Henri Lefebvre, *The Production of Space*, trans. Donald Nicholson-Smith (Oxford: Blackwell, 1991), 145.

tent into form can destroy it and so open up the way to innovation."[5] In many ways, this passage would epitomize a major shift in design thinking, opening avenues of innovation to other possibilities, other uses, and other contexts.

5. Ibid.

While Lefebvre articulated more overarching principles governing an understanding of everyday life, de Certeau, a sociologist and historian, took a more specific and ethnographic approach. His investigations into the realm of routine practices, or the "arts of doing" such as walking, talking, reading, dwelling, and cooking, were guided by his belief that despite repressive aspects of modern society, there exists an element of creative resistance to these strictures enacted by ordinary people. In *L'invention du quotidien* (*The Practice of Everyday Life*), de Certeau outlines an important critical distinction between strategies and tactics in this battle of repression and expression. According to him, strategies are used by those within organizational power structures, whether small or large, such as the state or municipality, the corporation or the proprietor, a scientific enterprise or the scientist. Strategies are deployed against some external entity to institute a set of relations for official or proper ends, whether adversaries, competitors, clients, customers, or simply subjects. Tactics, on the other hand, are employed by those who are subjugated. By their very nature tactics are defensive and opportunistic, used in more limited ways and seized momentarily within spaces, both physical and psychological, produced and governed by more powerful strategic relations.

Importantly, de Certeau shifts attention to acts of consumption, or use, and away from the historical preoccupation with the means of production. In so doing he focuses, for example, not on authorship but on reading, not on urban design but on walking through the city, not on theories of language but on the provisional and improvisational aspects of conversation. For de Certeau, consumption is not merely empty or passive, as many critics claim, but can contain elements of user resistance—nonconformist, adaptive, appropriative, or otherwise transgressive tactics—that become creative acts of their own fashioning. By locating such creativity in the user and beyond the conventional role assumed by the designer, de Certeau opens the possibilities of a design attuned to its use, context, and life rather than only its material quality, prescribed functionality, or formal expression.

While de Certeau saw the potential for individual acts of imaginative consumption, Perec enthusiastically wrote about a more poetic reimagination of everyday life. He was a member of the literary group OuLiPo, which was an affiliation of mathematicians and writers interested in producing poetry using systematic methods and agreed-upon constraints. One of his most famous literary contributions in this regard was *La Disparition* (*A Void*), a three-hundred-page novel that did not use a single word with the letter "e." His embrace of the quotidian can best be gleaned from the work *Espèces d'espaces* (*Species of Spaces*), a selection of ruminations on urban and domestic realms. Perec's literary inventiveness and poetic sensibility pervade the texts, which consider subjects such as the space of the page, the functionality inscribed by the rooms of a typical apartment, and the social life of a street or neighborhood. In the essay "Approaches to What?", he coins neologisms such as the "infraordinary" (versus the extraordinary) or the "endotic" (as opposed to the exotic) in order to discuss the specific character of the everyday. Most importantly, he obliges the reader to question the commonplace things that become habitual:

6. Perec, 210.

7. Ibid.

8. Perec, 31.

> "What we need to question is bricks, concrete, glass, our table manners, our utensils, our tools, the way we spend our time, our rhythms. To question that which seems to have ceased forever to astonish us. We live, true, we breathe, true; we walk, we open doors, we go down staircases, we sit at a table in order to eat, we lie down on a bed in order to sleep. How? Where? When? Why?"[6]

Perec's lists of possible inquiries and subjects for consideration are the very stuff of everyday life, the objects around us, the places we inhabit, the habits we form, the routines we perform. He asks such seemingly simple questions as "What is there under your wallpaper?"[7] Or he imagines an apartment that is organized around the senses instead of rooms: "We can imagine well enough what a gustatorium might be, or an auditory, but one might wonder what a seeery might look like, or a smellery or a feelery."[8] His poetic inquisition of the everyday affords design an opportunity to reimagine itself and to engage the world in new and inventive ways. Interestingly, two designs appear to respond to Perec's questioning, although not intentionally. Gis Bakker's *Peep Show* wallpaper produced under the auspices of Droog Design in the early 1990s was a blank white surface with large circles cut out, exposing the wall beneath and thereby reversing its conventional function. Architects Annette Gigon and Mike Guyer recently completed the design of a museum for an archaeological site in Germany where in A.D. 9 the Teutons defeated the Romans. Their design also includes three pavilions, "seeing," "hearing," and "questioning," which are devoted to different sensorial experiences. One space functions as a camera obscura and another, through a moveable acoustical pipe much like an ear trumpet, amplifies the sound of the surrounding fields, while a third transmits televised news broadcasts from around the world — stories that too often carry headlines of contemporary armed conflicts. Each space serves to underscore in a distinct way the visitor's perception of the site where an ancient battle once took place.

Design and Everyday Life

While the everyday has played an important role within modern art and the social sciences, it has only recently become central to discussions of design gaining momentum over the last decade. This tardiness seems implausible given that design, in its most basic sense, always already implicates itself in the construction of the everyday world. Yet, it is one thing to be part of the everyday—to help create it—and quite another to make it the subject of analysis or even critique. It is not coincidental that the quotidian should be of interest just as contemporary consumer culture is even more intricately woven into all aspects of daily life.

Among designers, interest in the quotidian is of course varied in its interpretations and responses. The nineties (and millennial) take on the everyday is different from earlier interests in anonymous or vernacular architecture, which saw such efforts as aspirational or inspirational— whether designers were learning from Venturi's Las Vegas or absorbing the lessons of Bernard Rudofsky.[9] These unschooled examples of design held some allure because they represented an untainted world that had existed

9. Robert Venturi, Denise Scott Brown, and Steven Izenour, *Learning from Las Vegas* (Cambridge, Massachusetts: The MIT Press, 1972). Bernard Rudofsky, *Architecture without Architects: An Introduction to Non-Pedigreed Architecture* (New York: The Museum of Modern Art, 1964).

independently of the discipline's increasing professionalization and before the expansive reach of commercial culture had taken hold. Seen through the professional's eyes, the vernacular attains an exotic status, while the commonplace fades from view. Today's everydayness is not reducible to period styles of the vernacular or the untrained informality of the anonymous. It accepts the bland, the generic, and the ordinary as the predominant context in which design will be situated, and against which the brand name and the spectacular operate.

Within architectural circles, interest in the everyday has taken on a particular meaning borne out of a reaction against the theory-laden 1980s, with its interests in the instruments of textual analysis, poststructuralism and, in particular, deconstruction, as well as an economic climate favorable to high-profile building in the 1990s.[10] Highly analytical, conceptually abstract, and predominantly textual in their focus, these theories were seen as too removed from actual lived experience, specific contexts, and practical constraints. Whether intended or not, such concepts were elastic enough to be adapted to intensive formal experimentation and innovation, and therefore provided a much-needed antidote to the regressive forms of most postmodernist design of the period. Not surprisingly, the opposing tack of the everyday would emphasize a renewed pragmatism, embracing specific conditions of use and actual social contexts. Following this shift, architecture is real, not abstract; it resists analysis and must be experienced, inhabited, and otherwise occupied. Against the rising cult of celebrity surrounding the architects of the 1990s building boom, the doctrines of everydayness advocate an antiheroic approach, opting to see architecture expressed as moments and cycles of habitation rather than in one-off monuments of expressiveness.[11]

Within the realm of product design, interest in everydayness can trace its development in the reaction to the design of the 1980s, with its elaborate use of materials and finishes and a hyper-styling of forms. Ventures such as Droog Design, a loose collective of initially Dutch designers who gained notoriety and influence in the design world in the early 1990s, typified this shift.[12] Embracing a renewed sobriety in the face of a resplendent materialism, Droog adopted a more straightforward attitude to materials, an

10. Steven Harris, "Everyday Architecture," in *Architecture of the Everyday*, eds. Steven Harris and Deborah Berke (New York: Princeton Architectural Press, 1997), 1–8.

11. Deborah Berke, "Thoughts on the Everyday," in *Architecture of the Everyday*, 222–226.

12. For an account of Droog Design, see *Droog Design: Spirit of the Nineties*, eds. Renny Ramakers and Gijs Bakker (Rotterdam: 010 Publishers, 1998).

23

13. See Ed van Hinte, ed., *Eternally Yours: Visions on Product Endurance* (Rotterdam: 010 Publishers, 1997) for discussions and strategies surrounding issues of product obsolescence and life cycle; and Conny Bakker and Ed van Hinte, eds., *Trespassers: Inspirations for Eco-Efficient Design* (Rotterdam: 010 Publishers, 1999) for a more lighthearted approach to sustainable design.

inventive approach to fabrication processes and methods, and a resistance to product styling. The attitude of Droog became defined by the latent humor and wit that characterizes so many of its products: a chandelier made from a cluster of eighty-five exposed lightbulbs, a chest of drawers created by strapping together a variety of used drawers, or a polyester-impregnated felt sink.

At the same time, a growing interest in ecology, sustainability, recycling, and product obsolescence fostered a change in attitude among many product designers that required a rethinking of previously held and unquestioned assumptions within the field about resourcefulness and wastefulness in production, the life cycles of products, and the role of use and consumption.[13] If product design was to be more than styling exercises, it needed to expand conceptually, explore new methods of fabrication, and be informed by the use, adaptation, and personalization of objects by users.

Without resorting to orderly definitions, this exhibition offers its own interpretation of everydayness and design. The assembled works are not recessive; they do not fade away into the familiarity of the world around us. Instead, these projects transform the ordinary into the extraordinary, acknowledging that the everyday is a participatory realm where design is essentially incomplete, knowing that people will eventually inhabit and adapt what is given. Collectively, these works are meant to challenge some basic tenets of design accepted in both public perception and professional preconceptions.

Strangely Familiar: Design and Everyday Life

The projects gathered together for this exhibition are a heterogeneous collection of distinctive works and unique ideas. They have been assembled to explore four themes related to the design of contemporary objects and spaces:

• polemical objects that force us to reconsider our relationship to products and dictate new rituals of use and expectations of performance

- portable structures that respond to nomadic conditions of lightness and ephemerality, thereby undermining long-held architectural principles of site-specificity and permanence

- multifunctional objects that change both shape and use, thereby blurring the traditionally fixed relationship between so-called "form and function"

- extraordinary designs that reference and transform otherwise ordinary objects and spaces, drawing our attention to everyday conditions

Rituals of Use

Many projects featured in *Strangely Familiar* attempt to implicate the user as a central figure or participant in a design's realization. The point is not to second-guess the consumer or to commodify formerly marginal activities, but rather to include user participation, personalization, customization, and even rejection as a vital element in the work. The incompleteness, openness, and unpredictability of such projects are in opposition to most ideals of design, which typically demand a high degree of finish and see adaptation as a flaw, or chance as a risk.

For designers the everyday represents the site of actual use—the messy reality where designs are negotiated. This is a realm beyond the carefully circumscribed boundaries of design proper; it is outside the client-designer commission or the controlled nature of test markets and focus groups. Critical theorists of the quotidian understand the everyday as a place where common practices and routines contain elements of dissent, subversion, or circumvention—small gestures or actions that were unanticipated, beyond the reach of the most carefully executed planning. Many designers now conduct field research to better understand how people use their products and services or to develop new products based on ad-hoc creations made by ingenuous do-it-yourselfers. However, these types of endeavors do not necessarily take a critical approach to design or reveal the underlying conditions of the everyday any more clearly. Such efforts are affirmative projects to the extent that they embrace existing conditions and situations but do not necessarily alter our relationship to everyday objects or challenge conventional ideas about design.

Countering this affirmative tradition of product design are works such those by Anthony Dunne and Fiona Raby, who engage in what they call "critical design." Operating outside of the traditional marketplace and the prescribed role of the professional product designer, they create simple-looking but conceptually complex objects in order to probe social behaviors and cultural values through long-term investigations. By doing so, they open up design to consider the effects of modern consumer products in our lives. Their *Placebo Project* (see pp. 90–106) explores our often anxious relationship to electronic goods through the creation of furnishings that can, for instance, detect the presence of electromagnetic radiation given off by modern conveniences such as laptop computers and cell phones. Although these objects perform a function, it is not one dictated by the market or demanded by a consumer. This reconsideration of the role of the designer and user is also present in the work of Michael Anastassiades. His *Social Light* and *Anti-Social Light* (see pp. 107–109), which brighten or dim in the presence of sound, are objects that respond to the behavior rather than the commands of the user. This reverses the conventional expectation about product servitude and consumer control and allows us to consider the effects that products have on the way we shape our lives. Both Dunne & Raby and Anastassiades utilize new technologies in order to augment existing forms, whether a table or a light, not to forward the idea of technological progress so closely associated with modern product design, but rather to interrogate this myth and consumers' expectations.

In a similar vein, the designers of *Dialog*—Marek Walczak, Michael McAllister, Jakub Segen, and Peter Kennard—explore the potential of digital technology to create alternative scenarios for computer-based experiences. *Dialog* (see pp. 110–113) counters the conventional notion of personal computing in which a single person interacts with the computer and perhaps with others online, but often alone and in isolation. Adopting the intrinsically social dynamics of a table as a gathering space, it allows multiple users to simultaneously explore a collection of ideas and artifacts.

If the consumer does have a role to play in the creation of products, it has been typically in the category of do-it-yourself (DIY) projects. In most cases, such endeavors are undertaken with a clear model in mind, something to replicate and emulate (think Home Depot classes or IKEA flat-pack furniture) These instructional offerings or kits-of-parts cast the role of the user as a form of deferred assembly labor. In more interesting variations of this approach, the design allows for some sort of uncertainty to take place in terms of the final product by centralizing the user as active and creative participant. This kind of open-ended resourcefulness can be seen in Blu Dot's *Free Play* shelving system (see pp. 114–119), which allows users to configure its parts in numerous ways, or in *Felt 12x12* (see pp. 120–125) by the studio www.fortunecookies.dk, which provides a basic module with which participants can create innumerable felted-wool garments and accessories.

Certainly user participation is the central premise behind the products of the design venture do create: a ceiling light that you swing from, providing illumination as well as exercise; a vase that can be thrown and cracked but not broken; and a chair made by smashing a cube of metal with a sledgehammer (see pp. 126–131). In the world of do create, consumer behavior is brought to bear in the realization of each product's function, thereby blurring the distinctions between creation and consumption. do create's humorous approach to design embodies deeper consumer desires to be released from the tyranny of perfection that surrounds product promotion and the frustration of so many failed and uncompleted DIY projects. Paolo Ulian's *Greediness Meter* (see pp. 132–135), an edible chocolate ruler, shares the playfulness of do create's approach but through an object whose own consumption is the measure of a guilty pleasure.

Traditional aspects of production and consumption in manufacturing industrial goods are actively rewritten by Tokyo-based elephant design. In a conventional marketplace, goods are offered to people for purchase in ways that try to predict what consumers may want. Using the Internet as its primary sales vehicle, elephant design proposes new products and solicits ideas from potential customers about goods they wish to purchase. Virtual models are created, manufacturing sources are identified, and sales prices are determined in advance. People can place an order for a product that will be produced when demand is sufficiently high to initiate its fabrication at an agreed-upon price. Among its many offerings is the *Insipid* collection of consumer goods (see pp. 136–144)—rice cookers, microwaves, cordless telephones, fax machines—with spare, minimal styling, pure white color, and refined detailing.

14. For more information on the history and development of portable structures and dwellings, see Dr. Robert Kronenburg, *Houses in Motion: The Genesis, History, and Development of the Portable Building*, second edition, (Hoboken, New Jersey: John Wiley & Sons, 2002).

Portability

Along with the city, the home is an important site in which to understand the workings of everyday life—its cycles of cooking, cleaning, sleeping, bathing, and eating, among others. It is the place where the strictures imposed by such things as social bureaucracy, science, and technology are felt most directly as an intervention in our personal lives. The home is synonymous with shelter, the nexus of our daily lives and, with increasing exception, a space that is distinct from the workplace. The house is a fundamental typology of architecture, one that ties us to a sense of place and personal history. This is true despite the fact that the typical American will move many times in a lifetime, changing jobs and homes along the way. This increased mobility is fueled in part by the expansion of technology that can keep us tethered to the office, if only virtually or remotely. The nomadic possibilities of contemporary life are explored in this exhibition through several projects that propose portable dwellings.[14] Not only do such structures acknowledge the desire for mobility and freedom, but they also confront our need for connection and community. The portable house also challenges long-held architectural assumptions of permanence and stability, which in turn account for the relatively low status such work has typically held. The most popular form of portable housing in the United States is the mobile home. Ironically, the vast majority of these dwellings rarely move about with the freedom associated with their portability. The trailer home's mobility is really a by-product of its prefabrication, simply a method of transport to its site, where it is permanently anchored.

The recreational vehicle embodies the freedom sought after by generations of retirees and vacationers whose migratory paths most closely recall the nomadic lifestyles of earlier civilizations. The popularity of the iconic Airstream, a trailer with a streamlined aluminum shell first introduced in the 1930s, is a testament to this quest for mobility. The Airstream provided the functions necessary for living but contained them in a package so lightweight and balanced that its publicity materials showed it being pulled by a bicycle. Of course, the Airstream was a product of the automobile culture and quickly became emblematic of the growing postwar market for leisurely pursuits. R&Sie...'s *Habitat Furtif* (see pp. 146–151), a living unit for one person, recalls the Airstream's metallic body with its highly polished reflective surface and its bicycle-powered transport. However, *Habitat Furtif* travels urban streets in search of safe harbor for its inhabitant rather than traversing the byways of the countryside in pursuit of recreational activities.

It is the distinction between permanent and temporary habitation that colors people's perceptions of portable housing. Typically understood as an acceptable solution for shorter periods of time, or in emergency situations, the portable home is seen by many as an escape from or loss of the everyday. For some, the need to maintain certain creature comforts, neatly captured in the expression "home away from home," too often means foregoing the conveniences associated with a sedentary lifestyle. For others the compactness, self-sufficiency, and convenience of mobile living outweigh the perceived loss of connection and community. The houses and structures featured in this exhibition represent a range of transience and permanence in dwelling.

While Markku Hedman's *Kesä-Kontti (Summer Container)* (see pp. 152–157) is designed for quick escapes to the woods, a kind of mobile weekend cabin, LOT-EK's *Mobile Dwelling Unit (MDU)* (see pp. 158–165) is envisioned as a permanent dwelling. Since the *MDU* is created from an existing shipping container, which is integrated into the worldwide systems for truck, rail, and ship transport, each unit is portable. LOT-EK envisions colonies of *MDU* harbors around the world, a structural framework that houses each person's unit, plugging into the necessary electrical and plumbing infrastructure—a kind of hotel in reverse, where occupants bring their rooms with them. While the *MDU* delights in its industrial and utilitarian roots, other designers have updated a modernist approach to the problem of the prefabricated home. Jennifer Siegal of the Office of Mobile Design (OMD) has developed several projects that utilize portable structures. OMD's *Portable House* (see pp. 172–179) is conceived of as a more flexible and ecologically friendly version of the conventional prefabricated home, but its modern styling and finishes resemble the Eames Case Study House more than the neighborhood trailer park. Like the *MDU*, *Portable House* can be situated in a variety of locations for permanent or temporary stays, but unlike the *MDU*, it can be configured with other portable houses to form courtyards or other common spaces for social and outdoor gatherings. This integrated and combinatory potential is also present in Markku Hedman's portable dwelling, *Etana* (*Snail*) (see pp. 166–171). Evoking its namesake, *Snail* consists of a hard exterior shell and a soft deployable membrane. Its internal components can be arranged by the user to create a variety of live-work configurations. Like OMD's *Portable House*, individual *Snail* units can also be connected to form larger spaces or communal environments.

While the previous projects rely on continuous mobility in order to maximize their functionality, other works explore portability as an extension of its ease of manufacture. For example, Alejandro Stöberl's *Prefabricated Wooden House* (see pp. 180–183) is trucked to its site, offering an economical alternative to more expensive conventional housing stock. Stöberl's elegant glass-box structure employs a series of wooden shutters along the length of the front and rear of the house that afford expansive views of the outside when open and privacy or protection when drawn. One can imagine *Prefabricated Wooden House* as a weekend destination, a modernist update to the country home. Shigeru Uchida's designs for a trio of teahouses (see pp. 184–187) are also prefabricated to facilitate shipping and relocation. Uchida's modernist update to the traditional teahouse includes translucent papers and perforated woods, lending to each structure the paradoxical feeling of both exposure and enclosure. Both projects are extensions of the conventional house, existing apart and distinct from it while still psychologically connected to the idea of a domicile, if only to escape it. Artist Alan Wexler creates works that explore the rituals and routines of life. His *Gardening Sukkah* (see pp. 188–193) is a portable structure that contains all the necessary implements and furnishings to celebrate the Jewish Sukkot festival of the harvest. The portability and transience of the sukkah signifies a historical connection to the life lived in the wilderness during the Jews' exodus from Egypt. The *Sukkah*'s collection of gardening tools, tableware, and cooking utensils evokes self-sufficiency, a veritable kit of parts uniting the cycles of growth, harvest, and consumption. Its hybrid form is part garden shed and part wheelbarrow, and with its retractable roof, table, and chairs it can be easily reconfigured to become the temporary outdoor dining area prescribed by religious tradition.

Another area of activity for portable structures is in the realm of emergency shelters used during various natural and man-made disasters. While most of these structures are by necessity of a basic or ad-hoc quality, architect Shigeru Ban's *Paper Loghouse* (see pp. 194–197) is a distinctive counterpoint. Originally used to shelter earthquake victims, *Paper Loghouse* employs commonplace, modest materials to great effect, creating a simple, functional, and beautiful structure that can be easily assembled by rescue volunteers and can endure for many months. Such a structure counters the vulnerability and transience associated with the tents used in such circumstances. The most elemental form of portable shelter is embodied in Martín Ruiz de Azúa's *Basic House* (see pp. 198–202). Weighing only a few grams, this metallic insulating cube can be carried in one's pocket and deployed on demand. While many of the previous projects express the potential for a more collective nomadic lifestyle, recalling perhaps the caravan, *Basic House* emphasizes the individual quest for maximum mobility and freedom.

Multifunctionality

The desire for portability corresponds to an interest in products with multiple functions, things that create efficiencies in space or weight, important considerations for mobility. After all, why take two things when one will do? Those of us with sedentary lives encounter this need when we choose to leave the comforts of home for a road trip or camping expedition and must decide what to take. What can be carried on one's back has always been the most reductive approach to this problem. Not surprisingly, garments are one locus of activity. While *Basic House* evokes the Basque sheepherder's tent/coat, a multifunctional garment that serves as a form of peripatetic shelter and bodily protection, Moreno Ferrari's *Tent* (see pp. 210–211) is the contemporary instantiation of this piece of clothing. Using simple tension rods, *Tent* can be formed from a translucent raincoat. Ferrari's designs for the Italian sportswear enterprise C.P. Company use modern materials and techniques. His ingenious creations for the aptly named *Transformables* collection include *Tent* as well as a cloak that converts into a kite (see pp. 205–209) or a jacket that becomes a sleeping bag (see pp. 212–213).

Multifunctionality has long been a characteristic of furniture design, particularly in circumstances where space is at a premium. A space for dining, the simple kitchen table is often the site of many functions, including the preparation of foods, a place for a child's study and play, or a surface for making crafts. In this instance, a piece of furniture is generic enough to suggest a multitude of activities. The modern equivalent is the storage unit, which, depending on its arrangement and location within the home, provides a place for clothes (wardrobe), linens (closet), dinnerware (sideboard), electronics (armoire), or collectables (cabinet). Multifunctional furniture is often a hybrid product, expressive of its dual functionality, such as the daybed or sofa bed. The eighteenth and nineteenth century witnessed a rise in the development of furniture based on the multiple components associated with machinery, such as the reclining or sleeping chair for train travel or the various schemes for integrated baths and kitchens. This represents a more complex approach of assembling different apparatuses into one unit.

The chair is perhaps the oldest and most developed form of furniture, one that closely maintains an intrinsic relationship to the human body. Perhaps not surprisingly, the variety of chairs is quite extensive, suggesting a range of sitting positions, from the informality of a stool to the upright posture of a dining chair to the repose afforded by the lounge chair. Julian Lion Boxenbaum's iconic *Rugelah Chair* (see pp. 214–218) captures in one piece of furniture a multitude of possibilities for sitting, lounging, and sleeping. *Rugelah Chair* explicitly references the form of rolled carpets often carried by nomads but is predicated on Boxenbaum's experiences using camping gear, products that put a premium on their functional efficiency. Similarly, Paolo Ulian's *Cabriolet/Occasional Table* (see pp. 219–221) is a sofa, storage unit, and coffee table in one. Both projects respond to the space limitations of small urban apartments and the highly mobile lifestyles of the young. These are but two examples of an increasing number of multifunctional furniture pieces produced with renewed enthusiasm today.

Implicit in multifunctional design is the idea of user choice, the ability to select the mode best suited to a particular situation. At an architectural scale, *Tumble House* (see pp. 222–227) is a six-sided structure designed by Koers, Zeinstra, van Gelderen of the Netherlands that allows people to rotate the building into six different positions, and each one changes the functionality of interior elements. For example, a door becomes a window or skylight. *Tumble House* behaves more like garden furniture, which can be rearranged, than conventional garden architecture such as the potting shed, the greenhouse, or the storage shed. New York–based su11 explores both prefabrication and mass-customization in *Composite Housing* (see pp. 228–232), which allows individualized components to be combined in multiple ways. These components, which replace traditional notions of rooms and spaces, can exhibit transitions on the same surface, indicating a different usage or programmatic change. Thus, materiality and texture become important design elements. By providing a variety of material and configuration choices to the consumer, su11 challenges one-off craft-based building traditions of architecture with fabrication techniques and industrial processes more akin to product design. This fundamental shift is possible largely because of changes precipitated by digital technologies for computer-aided design and manufacturing as well as the advent of the Internet.

These explorations of multifunctionality express a desire to provide multiple choices for users, allowing functions to be situationally contingent. The multifunctional object displays intrinsically hybrid formal qualities at odds with the conventional design philosophy of "form follows function." Coined by architect Louis Sullivan around the turn of the twentieth century, this expression became one of the guiding principles of modern design, one that continues today. Since the multifunctional object changes both shape and use, it complicates the otherwise tidy equation that a product's (static) form would be expressive of its (singular) function. The philosophy of functionalism is rooted in ideas like those espoused by Horatio Greenough, who wrote *Form and Function* in the early nineteenth century. Drawing upon examples of quintessentially American "no-nonsense" approaches to the design of everyday things, he countered the more ornamental style of Victorian England. Pointing to the design of industrial objects and structures such as the truss bridge, Greenough saw a natural affinity with the more scientific and objective ideas of engineering than he did with the artisanship associated with the craft guilds of Europe. By the early twentieth century, the philosophy of functionalism dominated the discourse of modern design, where it slowly ossified, becoming as static as the objects it produced. Ironically, it was the nineteenth century that witnessed great activity in the development of multifunctional objects, eschewing the role of the objective scientist or engineer in favor of the ingenuity of the inventor or the pragmatism of the tinker.

Transforming the Everyday
Lefebvre once wrote rhetorically, "Why wouldn't the concept of everydayness reveal the extraordinary in the ordinary?" His question is inverted through this exhibition, which asks instead if the concept of everydayness can reveal the ordinary in the extraordinary. Many projects embody the everyday only to transform it, giving it back to us anew. We witness this alchemy in works such as Jurgen Bey's *Kokon Chair* (see pp. 239–241), with its protective polyester-resin coating covering the ghostly presence of the ordinary chair that lies beneath, or in Atelier Bow-Wow's *Moth House* (see pp. 234–238), whose polycarbonite shell preserves a fragile domicile within. The tactic of surprising displacement, making the familiar strange, is at the heart of Doug Garofalo's renovations of typical suburban houses such as the *Markow Residence* (see pp.242–248), which give once-staid structures and homogenous forms an alternative spatial arrangement and appearance through complex geometry. Sometimes it is absence of an object that paradoxically brings forth its presence in the world, such as artist Rachel Whiteread's *Daybed* (see pp. 249–251) for London-based furnishings com-

pany SPC, which recalls the impression of a bed's mattress and frame, or Nucleo's *Terra: The Grass Arm-chair* (see pp. 252–255), seating that emerges from the lawn.

The transposition of scale, making the small large and the large small, is an important device in altering our perceptions of the everyday. The play of scale between the visible and the invisible can be gleaned in Marcel Wanders' *Airborne Snotty Vases* (see pp. 256–261), which transform the microscopic forms of mucus produced by a sneeze into an unexpected function. Constantin and Laurene Leon Boyms' series of miniatures, *Buildings of Disaster* (see pp. 262–277), makes the monumental tangible at a scale that can be possessed even if the events that took place there cannot be fully grasped. In this way they function like souvenirs, not models, because they do not reference the buildings per se but the stories that accrue to them. Constantin Boym's *Upstate* series (see pp. 278–284) takes the form of souvenir plates whose vistas do not depict famous travel sites but ordinary scenes of rural New York. In these vignettes, the commonplace has been elevated to a status typically reserved for the ceremonial and the commemorative—an unexpected subject in a familiar form.

It has been said that the daily life of a people can be seen through newspaper reportage. But the news, as Lefebvre duly noted, is in fact the compilation of extraordinary events, everything but the ordinary. Jop van Bennekom's *RE–* magazine (see pp. 285–295) eschews the typical news fare of media events and the personification of celebrity, both of which form the basis of most publishing, in favor of capturing the attitudes of ordinary people, even if the subject flirts with topics close to advertising, such as sex and boredom. *RE–*'s use of photography owes something to the informality of the snapshot but retains a strong directorial presence, orchestrating the actions and technical elements to great effect, in essence restaging the everyday with a certain artifice in mind.

The problem of designing or studying the everyday is precisely the tension between its reality and its inevitable artificiality. In other words, when the concreteness or realness of everyday life is the subject of study or the intention of design, it becomes instead a kind of second nature—a reference to the real, a depiction of the ordinary, an allusion to the commonplace. Certainly nature is one such sphere where interventions by humans are immediately perceived to create a secondary effect, even if these changes are eventually effaced in our minds.

Nature is under constant transformation by humans who create hybrid realms—an artificial nature. Perhaps it not surprising that a Dutch architectural practice would harness that country's reputation for altering the course of nature (in particular, its elaborate system of reclaiming land from the sea) as the basis for its design of a national pavilion. MVRDV's pavilion for *Expo 2000* (see pp. 296–299) takes the elements of the Dutch landscape and dramatically stacks them. The pavilion becomes a microcosm of the Netherlands—a compact reduction of the tourist destination that the country itself carefully cultivates. The shift of scale between the local and global conditions of farming, the original form of artificial nature, is expressed through two projects, *Scrambled Flat* and *Pig City*. R&Sie...'s proposal *Scrambled Flat* (see pp. 306–311) takes as its subject the Alpine village of Evolène, Switzerland, with its age-old approach to small-scale local farming and vernacular structures that house both humans and animals. MVRDV's *Pig City* (see pp. 300–305), predicated on the health and sustainability issues of corporate pork production, proposes large-scale, vertical pig farms. While both share a futuristic vision of millennial agriculture, including more vertically integrated forms of living and farming, they do so in distinctly different terms at vastly different scales.

Conclusion

The premise of this exhibition subverts the expectation of ordinariness and anonymity implied in evoking terms such as "design" and "everyday life." This is necessary in a world in which the definition of everyday life is no longer agreed upon or even understood in the way it was originally conceived. Implicit in this strategy is the idea that design can be attuned to the nuances of the quotidian without sacrificing innovation, inventiveness, novelty, or newness. Some have argued for a kind of anonymous or vernacular design firmly embedded in the landscape of everyday life as the only acceptable alternative to the kind of conspicuous design that has emerged so strongly over the last decade. Indeed, there are many people who subscribe to such an ideal for design, whether a self-effacing architecture so enmeshed in its context as to be barely noticeable or an outright rejection of material culture altogether. However, these strategies of mimesis and negation leave little room for design's creative energies or quest for invention. The projects featured in this exhibition stand out and apart from what we would call ordinary life. By doing so, they perform a self-reflexive action, causing us to reconsider our expectations of design and our approach to living, offering a provocative counterpoint to the habitual, the routine, and the commonplace. The exhibition intentionally spans multiple fields of practice and includes designers from many different countries whose projects vary in scope and scale. This range of people, ideas, and works is meant to reflect the intrinsic complexity of contemporary design. Some works offer themselves to the world as products to be purchased, while others exist as proposals; nevertheless, all contain compelling ideas that make us think about the world differently, in both large and small ways. The constancy and fluidity of the everyday ensures that it will continue unabated, but not unaffected. Design's task is to make us more aware of its effects, reconciling the growing predictability of design's conspicuousness—the familiarity of the strange—by disrupting its inevitable absorption into the everyday—the strangeness of the familiar.

Andrew Blauvelt is Design Director at the Walker Art Center in Minneapolis. As a practicing graphic designer he has received numerous professional awards and has published and exhibited widely. A critic and historian, Blauvelt has authored essays and guest-edited special issues on design and culture for many publications, including *Emigré, Eye, Visible Language*, and the *American Center for Design Journal*.

AARON BETSKY

THE STRANGENESS OF THE FAMILIAR IN DESIGN

Unfamiliar Design

The things produced under the sign of architecture and design seem alien to most people's daily lives. That is strange in itself, because the buildings and environments in which we live have either been designed by architects or formed according to the aesthetic or organizational rules of that discipline. Similarly, we all use objects, images, and spaces that have been designed to be efficient, convenient, comfortable, and maybe even beautiful. Yet we experience such things—when we notice them—as existing outside of our lives. At best, we see them as good slaves to our desires or, paradoxically, as fetish objects that awaken those desires. We want our houses to be comfortable, and perhaps to increase our status, and we aspire to ever larger and grander ones. We do not really need that new pair of shoes, but feel they will be easier on our feet, look better with our clothes, or are finely crafted, and, well, we simply must have them. The odd thing about design is that it is so familiar, yet its logic is so strange to us.

To a large extent, this is because we do not make the most of the objects, images, and spaces we use. We have to use them, and sometimes we even enjoy doing so, but they are not us. Their preexisting quality is something we take for granted and ignore, and their mass production gives them a particularly unexceptional status. Advertising turns them into lust objects; at the risk of sounding sexist, it is the material version of the Madonna/whore problem: We do not want to think about design in this way because it reveals a certain inadequacy in ourselves.

It is not all our fault. Designers have made their work inaccessible to our understanding of it and unfamiliar because they have a hard time being clear either about what they do or simple in what they make. Since we cannot do much about the basic economic and social structure of our society, it might be worth looking at why designers have made things difficult, and ask how they could try to use their skills to break through the barriers between ourselves and the objects we use. The idea might be to produce items that are not ideal but normal and clear. This happens when designers work to create something "simple." Such objects have the paradoxical effect of making us aware of the artifice all around us: they are strangely familiar.

The Design of the Unfamiliar

In the past, making something simple and revelatory would not have been easy. The designing disciplines may even be constitutionally incapable of making just the right thing. Design is the act of adding value to objects, images, and spaces to transform them from raw resources to useful phenomena. A car is produced and sold, but it is the designers who give it form, arrange the components, and create the image to be traded, thus clothing the everyday and useful with shiny new skins. Exactly because of the care put into making them, designed things are prestigious, expensive, beautiful, and alien.

Having or making designs for something is by its nature a sophisticated endeavor. It means not accepting things as they are, but wanting to either improve them or make them one's own. Designers do this for a variety of reasons. First, they want to make our lives easier. The very notion of a tool implies design, both in its manufacture and in its ability to transform one's environment. A hammer or a chisel creates a relationship between the human body and the world so that we can change our environment, and thus the tool must be designed so that it responds to our curves, muscles, and eyes while being able to affect the things on which it operates. Design is thus neither the human body nor the world, but it is what we make to create a relationship between those two. Design gives objects an autonomous shape or appearance.

Second, designers want to propose a better world, believing that with the help of tools, we can improve our environment. We can keep the rain and the sun out, we can keep ourselves warm, but we can also enter into a relationship with forms, spaces, and images that are more ideal. The designer offers us abstracted versions of what we see. Buying that car will somehow make us better, not just more comfortable or earlier at work. How and what this "better" is remains open to interpretation, and usually only designers can define that value to be gained from their labor. It seems that designers prefer to create something abstract and alien, precisely because it denies their contributions and opens the object, image, or space to multiple interpretations. Somehow, at least in modern design, smoothness, emptiness, clarity of line, and openness are meant to reflect our inner mental processes. Paradoxically, the appearance of the design gains in its ability to evoke such internal processes with the increased sophistication of its surfaces and form. The more the designer manages to represent nothing in the most fully realized manner, the more it appears to be approaching some truth.

The result of such associations and processes is that we do not assimilate the designed object, space, or image. Rather, it presents an alien and highly finished picture. One could just say that this means designers want to make things that are beautiful. The guilty pleasure of any designer is the ability to manipulate material and form to the point at which beauty appears—to the eye, the hand, the body, and maybe even the ear or the nose. The difference between design and what we call art is not only that design has a different social status, but that it is essentially a tool that connects the body to the world around it. Design can have a more visceral connection to the human body while retaining a relationship with what we think of as the wonders of nature.

All three of these criteria—ease, improvement, and beauty—have been used for millennia to justify the designer's work. Many derivatives have appeared, ranging from streamlining objects so as to increase sales acceptance to the notion of a classical or modern language of architecture. In all cases, however, the value of design remains in question, a situation we find reflected in the dubious position design holds as a discipline: Is it a craft or an art? Should it be part of engineering or aesthetics? And why in the hell should one pay for it? Things should just work and yet we want them to be beautiful, and designers have to navigate between our (and their own) conflicting goals.

Automatically Familiar Design

In the last few decades, designers have begun to develop strategies to justify their own activities as a response to developments in art theory that question the exact nature of beauty as well as the goal of the art object in relationship to its efficacy. They have also been influenced by threats of automatization of everything from production to design (everybody can now "design" a Web page, and most buildings are not designed by architects anymore). The simplest of these methods involves design as deeply as possible in processes of production and consumption. The most radical strategies move into the realm of what we might call art, where we are asked to become conscious of the world through design.

At its most basic, design seeks to become part of the infrastructure of everything made by human beings. We can see this on the smallest scale in the fields of nano- and biotechnology, where scientists talk about computer or gene architecture and designer drugs. Thus they indicate that, in the arrangements of elements at atomic and molecular levels, science directly influences and even designs the most fundamental elements of life. This might soon result in our altering the human body and the environment we inhabit in such far-reaching ways that we will redesign reality as we know it.

This is not so far-fetched. We have of course been engineering livestock and plants for millennia, and the Earth is by now largely shaped by humans. In addition, we have been using prosthetic devices for those same millennia, and they have been moving further and further into an intrinsic relationship with the body. How far is it from spectacles to pacemakers or artificial knees to organically grown livers? What has emerged now, for both scientist and designer, is a question of appearance. Technology has made the bio-things we design so small and has buried them so deeply in the processes of life generation that they have become invisible. We can no longer directly experience the products of design. Paradoxically, these deep interventions alter the biotopes and biomass to such an extent that the organism in the end appears slightly different. Frankenstein's monster might have been a science-fiction dream and the East German swimmers an aberration, but we are beginning to see more signals of human and other bodies that have been tweaked, twitched, and pulled to change their reality. Cyborgs might be way in the future, but how different am I from them when I switch from glasses to contact lenses to laser surgery, or if I ever get a chip embedded to regulate my chemical processes by delivering measured doses of drugs into my bloodstream?

This is the first way in which design becomes strangely familiar—by producing not the alien others, the mute objects of tools, buildings, or signs, but rather ourselves, our neighbors, our fields, and our air. Only occasionally do we notice that something somehow is different, out of the ordinary. Good designers play on this realization and produce prototypes that make us aware of this strangeness.

In architecture, this intrinsic form of design expresses itself in the growing involvement of designers with infrastructure projects as well as in their obsession with their role as part of the regulation of goods and data. There are simple reasons for this. Architects go where the money is, but are only used by that money when it needs to express itself. Otherwise, engineers of various sorts put together buildings such as warehouses or office blocks with much more ease. In our society, fewer and fewer people can afford to commission their own homes, or companies their own corporate headquarters. Only the state, which is losing the rationale for most of its other services as well as its ability to project its power through force or nationalism, needs architects to represent itself. In a concrete manner, this means the state employs architects to give shape to its most basic tasks—which increasingly focus on providing infrastructure—as symbols or icons. This is especially true in Europe, where cultural infrastructure (museums and multipurpose "event spaces") is now joined by road works, high-speed trains, airports, and especially bridges, and the bravura moments they engender as locations for the most self-evident architecture.

The results can look pretty strange. There are bridges such as the Erasmusbrug in my hometown of Rotterdam, which unfolds from the sidewalks and roads on either side of the Maas River to rise up into a single, leaning, baby-blue pylon that in its abstraction has become the city's most-used icon. But even the kinds of structures one could formerly point to as the objects of state power, such as museums, are disappearing underground (the Louvre, for example) or becoming an enigmatic unrolling of the urban landscape into a cultural facility (Zaha Hadid's urban carpet concept for the Contemporary Arts Center, Cincinnati).

Some architects are even exploring the meeting place between concrete and organically formed infrastructure. The so-called blobsters, led by Greg Lynn, Lars Spuybroek, Foreign Office Architects, and several other architects working across the globe with the same software and philosophy, argue that if one attaches the act of architecture to the production and manipulation of code, one can develop forms that might appear profoundly strange, but are complexly intrinsic to the way things are made or grown. The largest built example of this manner of working is the Yokohama Ferry Terminal, completed in 2002 using a design by Foreign Office Architects that represents exactly the merger of computer programs and the state's production of a large-scale infrastructure. To the architects of the Erasmusbrug, Ben van Berkel and Caroline Bos, architecture exists "between art and airports"; it is the organization of complex forces at the level of infrastructure and through the manipulation of data input and output, but results in the creation of something we might call art: an icon, a symbol, something strangely familiar.

Taking this approach one step further, a new generation of designers is focusing only on the collection and manipulation of information. These data miners range from graphic designers such as Bruce Mau and Erik Adigard to architects such as MVRDV. To them, the activity of design is first and foremost an act of gathering available knowledge about their world. Since we have now come to the conclusion (or at least some scientists and philosophers agree among themselves) that the only truth is probable or statistical, these designers act at the level of what can be known. Like the successful and often-copied compilers of the *Harper's Index*, they surf the Internet and libraries of the world for the most absurd and the most banal facts and figures, and then find ways of giving this data form. With the use of new computer visualization tools, they can create a whole architecture out of this information. In projects such as *MetaCity/DataTown*, MVRDV makes "datascapes" that show landscapes of information through which one zooms with effortless ease on a trip into a not-so-distant future. On this journey, the amount of garbage (though not the stuff itself) becomes a mountainous landscape of the words for its various components ("refrigerators," "compost") piled on top of each other. The architects even let dancers loose in these projections to create a performance called *Manyfacts*.

In so doing, MVRDV and its fellow miners come close in their electronic pragmatism to crossing over into the world of advertising. This is the reverse side of the way in which design is involving itself as deeply as possible in the processes of producing the real, i.e., the products, places, and images we should buy as the possible result of a manipulation of data. If one descends to the level of code, after all, one can produce not only new and strange shapes or images but also build the normal, the familiar, and the ordinary better, faster, and more efficiently. Computer-controlled milling devices produced not only the panels for the Guggenheim Bilbao but millions of ornate cuckoo clocks in China. The trick is to make the completely artificial appear utterly normal. The most frightening (and entertaining) example of this was the film *The Matrix*, which in 1998 promised us a banal reality—which looked exactly like the office cubicles and subway stations we already knew—but was no more than a three-dimensional projection to make us feel at home.

Designers have been counterfeiting reality for centuries, making flat ceilings look like endless skies or giving Naugahyde the appearance of leather. Nowadays they have become so successful that it is often impossible to see the difference between the real and the artificial: in fact, there is no original for objects or images produced on the computer. Designers sell these products of zeros and ones as merely the normal, familiar stuff all around us. This is the other side of branding, image building, and mass customization that supposedly makes our economy more and more dependent on design. Those Gap or Levi's jeans have to be designed to look like the jeans we already know, and yet they are made with increasingly sophisticated techniques to save money and give us the sense that they are not alien. You can even have them form-fitted to your body with a laser-scanning device.

The Strange Case of the Vernacular

Such developments in both production and consumption are not driven only by the logic of how we make and sell things. There seems to be—though it is difficult to trust the endless studies and reports that marketing firms produce—a growing need for the familiar, the known, the old, and the unthreatening. People want to live in the house they imagine their parents grew up in, they want hammers that look old-fashioned even if they have ergonomic grips, and they want to believe through packaging that their food really comes from pristine, unadulterated fields. They want what in American architecture is called the vernacular.

The word has no direct translation in other Western languages, or even really in British English. It first came into use after the Civil War, when Americans began to self-consciously invent a culture to go along with the nation they had built. The vernacular denoted the houses and spatial arrangements (both in the interiors and in the fields around the buildings) that had always been there, that had been made by hand, and that represented a way of doing things that human beings had laid down over centuries and perfected through use. The traditional New England home was to be the veritable "home, sweet home" because of the memories that adhered to it, and because it was built out of local materials by local craftsmen in a manner that was particularly suited to the climate and the inhabitants' way of life.

By now these modes have become tropes and then standard building practice, so that most American suburban developments today let buyers choose between variations on neo-Georgian models with such labels as

"Washington," "Jefferson," "Madison," and often, strangely, "Lincoln." The same is true for product design, offering stoves, refrigerators, and other kitchen implements that look and work like historic types. The problem becomes immediately evident here: such items were new and alien when they first appeared less than a century ago, and the same is true for the houses, which were plunked down on the recently cleared fields of New England according to plans imported from England in the seventeenth century. As a result, the new/old things and images look fake and alien.

The logical corollary to this argument is that the ultimate vernacular would be invisible. It would be, as landscape historian J. B. Jackson has pointed out, no more than a sod hut constructed out of the material right around it, barely sticking out of the ground. Any importation or manufacturing of material (including cutting trees into planks), or any application of organizational or aesthetic principles, would pull the house from the realm of vernacular and into that of design. What in the United States is called vernacular is thus actually a high-class imposition of an idea about how one should live and use space. It is a rather high-level representation of the image of the individual who commissions, designs, or owns the building or space.

The same is true for images and objects. The more designers try to find "authentic" typographic styles or go back to "natural" arrangements of pages, or the more they come up with "retro" cars meant to evoke the innocent speed at which we used to move down the highway, the more these concoctions seem far-fetched and alien to us. We try to solve this unease by importing "vernacular" objects from other cultures: Andean rugs, adobe building technology, and Japanese tableware are popular because we sense an authenticity in these things. Yet there they sit, alien intrusions in unfamiliar domestic landscapes, divorced from the place and logic with and in which they were produced and sold.

Maybe this is enough. It could be that the job of the designer is to do no more and no less than to shape or form (design) the objects, images, and spaces of everyday life into the familiar. No matter how our houses, our cars, our hammers, and our magazines are produced, and no matter how we are persuaded to buy them, if we can believe they are authentic, simple, and pure, that might be enough. A magazine called *Real Simple* wants to persuade us of this idea. The many do-it-yourself home supply chains and the publications that support them are part of this wish to live in a dream of natural production and consumption.

The New Familiar
The strangely familiar might thus be that which is plastic but appears real. It might be that which has a familiar form but works in sophisticated ways. It might be the electric blanket, the athlete on designer drugs, the eyelids filled with Botox, or the burled-wood panel stretched over the car's microchips. That does not mean it is all *retardataire*: it is also the look of abstraction, simplicity, and clarity that held sway in fashion during the 1990s, persuading us to believe that Prada's outrageous prices were justified by craftsmanship and the fact that they were, somehow, just right. The strangely familiar may also come from the desire for the pure that still pervades much of the marketplace. Making it real, making it simple, making it true, and making it pure might mean only making it look that way. The strangely familiar might only be strange in its familiarity that is so fundamentally artificial.

But there is another way of making the strangely familiar. Designers have been worrying about their position for more than a few years now, and many of them refuse to accept the disappearance of what they do into something that is supposed to look different than it is. To them, the strangely familiar is exactly that which makes us aware of how strange the familiar is. It is, to paraphrase the French philosopher Jean-François Lyotard, the act of presenting the impossibility of faithful representation within representation itself.

Such attitudes are already implicit in the kind of work described here. Neither Greg Lynn nor MVRDV, neither graphic designer Erik Adigard nor the maker of ergonomic tools Tucker Viemeister, believe they are disappearing into machine logic. Rather, they think, whether consciously or not, that they are revealing the internal contradictions of the situation in which they are working. By making the presence of data explicit, we can become aware of the power it has over our lives. By showing us what will happen if we do not control this data, we can experience a counter-model to what we might think of as the less-than-desirable future of complete, uncontrollable, and unknowable artificiality.

This is the realm of science fiction, of attitudes toward technology that date back to the Arts and Crafts movement of the mid-nineteenth century. Often seen as celebrating the fictitiousness of craft and the vernacular, it was also the movement in which thinkers such as William Morris and John Ruskin and designers such as C.R. Ashbee pleaded for the use of machines and even man-made materials so that we could understand their very artificiality. Frank Lloyd Wright argued for using the mechanized lathes and saws that then dominated the furniture industry, not to create ornament that would cover the object, but to dig into the wood, revealing its grain and texture.

The notion that we can reveal the substrate of the real by using the artifice of mining, cutting, removing, and simplifying is completely inherent to most notions of modern design we might call avant-garde or simply modernist in their desire to disclose their own artifice. Ornament was a crime to the architect Adolf Loos, not just because it attracted dust and looked ridiculous, but because it was a lie. Design should be a way of wiping out the falsehood of modern life and revealing its internal contradictions. Whether this would lead to a situation in which our own sense of irreconcilability with a receding base reality would become conscious (so that we would at least all be functioning schizophrenics or neurotics) or whether this act of revelation would assuage our fears by allowing us to understand them remains unresolved and a matter more for psychoanalysts and philosophers than for designers.

The Newly Strange

Until now, this stripping, revealing, and confronting us with reality has not produced utopia, and the failure of that perfect world to arrive has led many designers to turn toward an opposite methodology, that of gathering, collecting, and assembling what was already around them. In modern art, this took the form of assemblage and collage, in which ready-made objects and images gained new meanings through their composition within a set frame. In this way, artists began to approach the world of the designer because the bits and pieces that made up their art were in general scraps of advertisements, tools, train tickets, and other objects of design. Their art was also that of the designer since they added value through assembly, composition, and legibility. After World War II, artists such as Jean Tinguely or the members of Fluxus even began to make constructions that were direct satires of the logical mechanisms designers used. Collage and assemblage shaded into a ludic form of criticism in which the absurdity of a designed world became evident.

With very few exceptions, until fairly recently designers failed to pick up on such attitudes. They were so bound up with the idea that they had to make things that worked that they never stopped to think about making objects, images, or spaces that looked liked they worked, but didn't. Similarly, the notion of packaging was so built into the nature of design that the idea of not forming and covering mechanisms with as simple and pure a shape as possible seemed absurd. Finally, the notion that one should create something as simple and pure as possible to help make the world better was alien to the world of hunting and gathering the artists now proposed. How could design possibly abrogate its role as making the world more useful, comfortable, and better while still revealing the nature of the world?

Only in the 1980s did some designers begin to pick up on a few hints of "hippy aesthetics" and the desire of architects such as Bernard Rudofsky or John Habraken to let people assemble their own homes out of available materials. Rudofsky and Habraken proposed that architecture and design might disappear into the assembly of prefound materials, thus producing forms that were ad hoc and always by their nature unfinished. Most architects and designers who joined the Peace Corps or tried to find a systematic way of creating such systems of assembly failed. On the other hand, architects such as Coop Himmelblau proposed architecture as the assembly of the kind of generic and flexible loft spaces that were the barely designed bass note of modern industrial capital production. These architects then lifted such generic spaces up on what they called the "long thin legs of architecture" that were matchstick-like groupings in which the various forces acting on a building, such as gravity, the weight of occupants, and the wind, were not subsumed into thick columns or walls, but rather each given their own constructional element. The act of coming up with the image, the new idea, receded to the level of a "psychogram," an indecipherable sketch they made with their eyes closed. There were no more diagrams or premeditations, only semiautomatic assembly.

Unfortunately, their work still looked strange, mainly because they gave the finished product a sense of fit and finish that denied the collagelike promise of their developmental models. In the 1970s Frank Gehry, working in California, took another approach. Deciding that "a building under construction is much more beautiful than when it is finished," he designed a series of homes in which the stud construction of wood posts and beams was (rhetorically, at least) left revealed. Elements from the surrounding environment then came into the building, including unfinished plywood, chain-link fencing, and corrugated plastic. The houses looked unfinished or still under construction, even though their composition was in fact carefully calibrated.

While Gehry quickly moved on to other modes of design, a whole group of designers in southern California picked up on some of the methods he had developed and turned them into the building blocks for something I have called, after the world's largest chain of home building-supply stores, "Home Depot Modernism." In general, one could say the methods used by this disparate group (which has at various times included Morphosis, Eric Owen Moss, Hodgetts & Fung Design Associates, Koning Eizenberg Architecture, and Rob Wellington Quigley) were also informed by the presence in the area of a long tradition of taking apart and tinkering with the products of mass production. "If the English 'high-tech' architects wear lab coats," Thom Mayne of Morphosis famously said, "we are the guys in dirty overalls lying under the cars."

Pieces of cars and airplanes, but also, and perhaps more appropriately, plumbing supplies, building hardware, electrical controls, and scrap metal all made their way into the buildings these architects assembled. At their best, as in Gehry's own house or in the Culver City office renovations by Moss, these structures looked as if the messy surroundings of the Los

Angeles flatlands had somehow been sucked onto a building site and there used by a distracted handyman to create a structure that had a clear and sometimes even rather grand coherence. That was the trick: these architects made the familiar not only strange but strangely beautiful, exactly because the compositional and functional logic the designers still used had become completely intrinsic to the form.

Architects in other parts of the United States, such as Smith-Miller + Hawkinson or Kennedy & Violich, developed their own methods of Home Depot Modernism. So did industrial designers such as John Dickinson, who began making furniture out of plumbing supplies, and graphic designers such as Tibor Kalman, who saw their work as the reuse of existing images, types, and forms rather than the production of slick new compositions. Yet somehow these forms of reuse always had a slightly imagistic quality, as if they were tricks the designers were using to make something that looked like a three-dimensional collage rather than an intensification of their surroundings into something strangely familiar. It seemed as if Home Depot Modernism needed to be able to mimic the familiar world in at least a slice of its totality in order to really be strange.

The designers who broke through this impasse assembled themselves in 1993 in a loose collective called Droog. This initiative of critic Renny Ramakers and jewelry designer Gijs Bakker pulled together a number of others whose work was in turn based on experiments by graphic designers such as the groups Hard Werken and Wild Plakken. These post-1960s designers had taken an antiauthoritarian spirit, an interest in the vernacular, and a concern for the environment and translated it into work that had the quality of collage and looked like propaganda. However, it was disciplined by a strong sense of proportion, legibility, and all other traditional attributes of good design, providing a familiar sensibility to the work. Droog designers saw their task as gathering objects on the streets and reusing them, with the designer adding only something invisible: the concept. Their work was successful because they also did not want to add either new forms or new ideas; they felt they should reuse those as well. The result was objects such as Piet Hein Eek's chests of drawers, for instance, which were more or less traditional in their shape, but consisted of various pieces of discarded furniture. Since neither image, type, nor material were new, the shock of the familiar assembled in a new manner was all the stronger.

The designers who produced objects under the Droog label utilized a variety of techniques to make the strangely familiar. Marcel Wanders dipped rope in a plastic resin to make a chair of conventional shape that seemed illogical to the eye and in its construction. Hella Jongerius combined rubber with fragments of old Delft blue crockery to create faux old vases. The degree of invention was matched only by the rigorousness with which objects found on the street were reused in unusual ways: sponges or condoms impregnated with clay to make vessels, bus advertisements turned into wastepaper baskets, hammers turned into coatracks. But Droog also played with our expectations, as when Ineke Hans turned out what looked like a roughly hewn table and chairs but was actually outdoor furniture made of plastic. Artifice trumps artificiality and turns it back on itself.

A generation of younger designers and architects is pursuing such ideas even further. They range from industrial designers who work in the Droog mode to architects such as LOT-EK in New York, who seem to have arrived by independent means at a similar working method that also folds into it many aspects of Home Depot Modernism. Here conceptual and material reuse meets the use and misuse of mass-produced or standard elements. The strangeness of the familiar is also beginning to intersect with a movement coming from the world of landscape design. Projects such as George Hargreaves' Guadalupe River Park in San Jose, California; Julie Bargmann's project for the tailings of an abandoned West Virginia coal mine; and Peter and Latz's North Duisburg Industrial Park in Germany are moving their discipline toward the creation of an artificial vernacular that consists of drainage and agricultural reuse plans combined with the slice-and-dice layering of collage to form landscapes that preserve the familiar but look almost surreal.

Come Back to the Raft, Huck Honey

All this work certainly has in common a "comeback effect." The essence of the strangely familiar would be that it holds up a distorted mirror to the world around us, giving us back the world as we thought we knew it, but in a more or less subtly altered form. This produces what the Germans call the feeling of the *unheimlich*, or "unhomely": one knows one is at home, but there is something basically and frighteningly wrong. This is a very different effect from that of the surreal, which reveals the monsters and perversions that may or may not be intrinsic to our lives and our bodies. Instead, this comeback effect reassures us that we are still here and everything is in its place, and yet invisibly alters the basic configurations.

In some ways, this brings us back to the most fundamental way in which design has found itself in strangely familiar territory. We are talking again about the invisible, the absolutely fundamental, the natural that has become artificial or vice versa, and the undecidability of reality. In the work of graphic designers such as Jop van Bennekom, or in artist Jorge Pardo's *4166 Sea View Lane*, a house as artwork, something is very wrong, but everything appears to be right. A kind of new banality results. Because the designer removes her- or himself so far from the process of making the object, image, or space, it is difficult to discern what is designed. Instead, the observer or user at first sees only a normal situation, and perhaps even one that seems slightly worn, clichéd, out-of-date, or even ugly. Building on the tradition of the purposefully ugly that modern artists have used to give their art a critical content, but also on the notion of the *informe*—the unfinished, formless, and gooey mess that one does not know how to handle—this kind of design challenges the very notion of presentation and utility that constitutes it as a discipline.

At its simplest level, this is design that shocks by misbehaving. It is in evident bad taste, as in Constantin Boym and Laurene Leon Boym's collectable souvenirs of sites of disaster (banal scale reproductions of venues of great horror, such as the World Trade Center), and thus makes us realize that we are complicit in the construction of ideas about what is good and bad. It perhaps even offends us, confronting us with colors (the

53

brown so popular in the 1970s is now back in vogue) or shapes that have uncomfortable associations, without ever being explicit about their references. This is also design that is clever. Rather than shouting out its difference or its identity, it waits, as if in a trap, until the potential shopper, unnoticing but troubled by something about that perfume bottle, turns around and concentrates on that strange piece of almost nothing. "That is the moment I live for," Gap personal products executive and designer Gary McNatton once said.

In all cases, the work has to be both strange and familiar to succeed. These "strange-makers" use some basic techniques. The first is to appeal directly to the human body, giving us back our own body in altered ways. This occurs most often in the areas of fashion and graphic design, where software such as Photoshop can make the blandest body look slightly strange—though certain artists, such as Orlan, surgically alter their bodies as artworks. The second technique is to give our environment back to us in ways that are changed, but invisibly so. This is the realm of architects and can be seen in the work of Neutelings / Riedijk in the Netherlands, who used an indoor atrium in a student center in Utrecht as a place to collect and recycle rainwater, and Diller + Scofidio in the United States, who used thousands of jets of water to make a pavilion as a cloud of mist for their *Blur Building* in Yverdon-les-Bains, Switzerland. The third is to alter the relationships between the body and its environment, as for instance Droog's do create commission did in 2000 by "inventing" such objects as a metal cube that the user has to hammer into the shape of a chair. Here the strangeness can occur only in the way one behaves or acts, and the only way we can know it is through documentation.

Taken together, these methods promise us a new world of design in which nothing will be the same. Sound familiar? Sound strange? It is, of course, the promise that is inherent in design. It will keep working on our world and on us, changing and making evident the relationships between ourselves, our bodies, other human beings, and our environment. It will do so by continually coming up with new ways of establishing and formalizing those relationships. It will, in other words, make tools, houses, images we can read, and other useful, comfortable, and idealized phenomena. It will now do so not with the explicit result of showing us a better world, or with the implicit goal of making that world better. This new form of design will try to disappear even as it becomes ever more ubiquitous, and will be ever stranger in its methods even as it looks ever more familiar. The strangely familiar is the brave new frontier of design and perhaps of how human beings can be conscious of the world they increasingly make in their image, even as that image becomes increasingly artificial.

Aaron Betsky has been Director of the Netherlands Architecture Institute in Rotterdam since 2001. Previously, he was Curator of Architecture, Design, and Digital Projects at the San Francisco Museum of Modern Art. He is the author of a dozen books, including, most recently, *Landscrapers* (London: Thames & Hudson, 2002) and *Three California Houses* (New York: Rizzoli International Publications, 2002). He lectures and writes about architecture and design.

JAMER HUNT

JUST RE-DO IT: TACTICAL FORMLESSNESS AND
EVERYDAY CONSUMPTION

A MUNDANE ITINERARY ON THE EVE OF TERROR

SOUTH PORTLAND, Me., Oct. 4 – For their last night on Earth, the pair of terrorists stayed at a Comfort Inn on a sterile strip of gas stations and fast-food joints here.

Driving a silver-blue rented Nissan Altima, Mohamed Atta and Abdulaziz Alomari spent at least part of the evening in the most pedestrian of pursuits, mostly along a broad suburban stretch of asphalt called Maine Mall Road: 15 minutes at a Pizza Hut, a quick stop at a gas station and about 20 minutes at a Wal-Mart. . . . They also stopped at two automated teller machines.

"They did nothing different than almost any other person who visits Maine from out of state," said Stephen McCausland, a spokesman for the Maine Department of Public Safety. "It is eerie to know that these two central figures in this horrific event were here doing those things the night before."

–The New York Times (October 5, 2001)

"They circulate without being seen, discernible only through the objects that they move about and erode. The practices of consumption are the ghosts of the society that carries their name."

–Michel de Certeau[1]

The space between the utter banality of the everyday and the cataclysmic eruption of September 11 is immeasurable. They exist on incommensurate scales. Comfort Inn, Wal-Mart, Pizza Hut, the ATM. Though we might cringe to admit it, these landmarks *are* the everyday for most people in twenty-first-century North American life. They are embarrassingly familiar. Their styles derive from lowest-common-denominator planning. Sav-Mart, Loaf 'n Jug, Pep Boys: they are strange, too; polymorphous, nonsense syllables clumped together and seared into our unconscious by enormous roadside signs, abrasive advertisements, and cloying jingles. They may not represent the apotheosis of Western civilization and yet they are—through their numbing ubiquity—the essence of our consumer society.

Between the Comfort Inn and the World Trade Center towers there stands an abyss, too, that illustrates the rupture between the monumental and the mundane. "To be lifted to the summit of the World Trade Center is to be lifted out of the city's grasp.... The World Trade Center is only the most monumental figure of Western urban development," wrote philosopher Michel de Certeau.[2] The towers emerged against the ground of the ordinary. They are vertical; Wal-Mart is horizontal. The twin towers were colossal symbols; the Comfort Inn thwarts memory. The World Trade Center was unique (even if twinned); Wal-Mart is everywhere. Between thrust and sprawl, we see the warp and weft of a consumerist *everyday*. This dialectic helps explain in some ways the hold that the Boyms' *Buildings of Disaster*, a series of miniatures depicting scenes of famous calamities, has for us. Its power comes from the compression of the extraordinary—monuments and disaster—into the ordinary— tchotchkes. It is the depths of the unbridgeable chasm between these registers that their work illuminates. Like figure and ground, the ordinary and the monumental are imperceptible without the other.

The common and the extraordinary intersect to form the matrix out of which the practices of design create the built environment. Design, unlike art, must locate itself within the ordinary. We engage design with all of our senses. The things we see and read, the objects we use, and the places we inhabit are covered by the fingerprints of graphic, product, and architectural designers. While these products do not comprise the world,

1. Michel de Certeau, *The Practice of Everyday Life* (Berkeley: University of California Press, 1984), 35.

2. Ibid., 92–93.

they do constitute increasingly large swathes of it. The built environment (a term I use to designate the combination of all the above design work) is the physical infrastructure that enables behavior, activity, routines, habits, and rituals. To evoke philosopher-social critic Michel Foucault, this is design as a disciplinary practice. The irony, however, is that while design generally furnishes this material support of the everyday in our culture, designers are incapable of designing the everyday. What I mean by that is not that designers lack the ability or the talent, but that the everyday is, as a phenomenon, inaccessible to the design process. Design can approach it, asymptotically, but it will never reach it.

The reasons for this are manifold. Designers cannot claim the everyday because as soon as they pull near to it, it evaporates. It is, as its name indicates, a temporal category. Everyday practices are aleatory and fugitive. They resist codification because their heterogeneity is both meaningless in its particularity and distorted when we abstract or generalize it. Art historian Deborah Fausch sums up the paradox this way: "The very act of labeling a part of experience as 'everyday' alters its fluid character and its immersion in an ongoing stream of events, substituting a hypostasized mental object formed according to the rules governing theoretical operations."[3] The everyday is what the act of analysis cannot comprehend. It is, to use philosopher Henri Lefebvre's term, the residuum, or what gets left over in the act of sociological scrutiny. One person's everyday is irrelevant, and everybody's everyday is unimaginable.

The temporality of everyday practices has elicited a range of recent design work that challenges the hegemony of a static, permanent design "product." These works embrace ideas of formlessness, decay, impermanence, abuse, misuse, and confusion.[4] They beg for connection and modification. They also refuse reduction to the typical categories of the beautiful or the useful. Rather than fetishizing the final product, these works engage design as process. While not pointedly political, they do raise questions about consumption and its politics—a rare gesture in product design, particularly. These works do not represent a sea change in the design disciplines, but they do intersect with the practice of everyday life in surprisingly novel ways.

3. Deborah Fausch, "Ugly and Ordinary: The Representation of Everyday Life," in *Architecture of the Everyday*, eds. Steven Harris and Deborah Berke (New York: Princeton Architectural Press, 1997), 78.

4. This idea of the "formless," borrowed from Georges Bataille, has a robust intellectual history. See Yves-Alain Bois and Rosalind Krauss, *Formless: A User's Guide* (New York: Zone Books, 1997) and Denis Hollier, *Against Architecture: The Writings of Georges Bataille* (Cambridge: MIT Press, 1989).

Time of the Everyday

What is the everyday? This simple question does not yield a simple answer. Sociological inquiry has struggled to come to terms with something so familiar and at the same time so elusive. In her overview of Lefebvre's work, Mary McLeod points out that:

> While it [everyday life] is the object of philosophy, it is inherently nonphilo-sophical; while conveying an image of stability and immutability, it is transitory and uncertain; while governed by the repetitive march of linear time, it is redeemed by the renewal of nature's cyclical time; while unbearable in its monotony and routine, it is festive and playful; and while controlled by techno-cratic rationalism and capitalism, it stands outside of them.[5]

Sociological methods are, by their very nature, pattern-seeking. Except for case studies, where a part stands in for the whole, it is never enough to recount the particular daily events of one individual's life. It would make no sense without the broader context of a culture's belief system, its ritu-als, its institutions, and its social structure. Instead, abstractions are made from a deep understanding of many different individuals' experiences, routines, and beliefs, all of which are boiled down and generalized in order to make a pattern of greater sense. To capture the everyday is ultimately — like Charles and Ray Eames' film *Powers of Ten*—a paradox of optical res-olution: too close and you can't see the forest for the humdrum and parochial trees (think Andy Warhol movies); too far away and you miss the trees for the large, undifferentiated mass of forest.

It was Lefebvre who made it clear that that conundrum was unresolv-able: the dialectic of the everyday could not be synthesized into a higher *truth*. As he argues, "Modernity and the everyday constitute a deep struc-ture that a critical analysis can work to *uncover*."[6] Lefebvre does put the everyday, however, into a historical context. It emerges concurrently with modernity. Or, to put it more accurately, the everyday as a *concept* emerges with modernity. We are able to discern its outlines only with the advent of industrial production, planned obsolescence, and the surpluses they gen-erated. As Lefebvre writes, "The everyday is therefore a concept. In order for it to have ever been engaged as a concept, the reality it designated had to have become dominant, and the old obsessions about shortages . . . had

5. Mary McLeod, "Henri Lefebvre's Critique of Everyday Life: An Introduction," in *Architecture of the Everyday*, 13.

6. Henri Lefebvre, "The Everyday and Everydayness," trans. Christine Levich with the editors of Yale French Studies, in *Architecture of the Everyday*, 37.

to disappear."[7] Those shortages were rendered meaningless in the economies of abundance and plenty that mass production created. A modern sense of time—as progress, unidirectional and linear—has pushed aside the preindustrial, cyclical experience of time (that of solstices, seasons, harvests, birth, and death). News, fashion, and design all bombard us with the message that time is moving ferociously forward. Two modalities of time commingle now, swirling in competing and confusing ways. We crave the new, we delight in change, and we bemoan the good old days. Part of our modern condition, as many have pointed out, is to learn to survive as the powerful current of time tows everything forward with it. We look for branches to grasp, things to hold on to, so that we can resist time's passing, even if just for a moment. We crave the illusion of stasis, yet we buy the latest in fashion (or at least feel the pressure to do so). The everyday, then, is an anxious oscillation between the gravitational poles of stasis and change.

Practices of Everyday Life

How do these forces affect individuals and the choices they have and make? In his reflections on everyday practices, de Certeau explores these dynamics through a conceptual framework of *tactics* and *strategies*. That he develops these two terms within the context of mass production and consumption makes them particularly salient to design. He is trying to uncover the ways in which individual members of society create certain freedoms within the inescapable net of late capitalist, consumer culture: "The thousands of people who buy a health magazine, the customers in a supermarket, the practitioners of urban space, the consumers of newspaper stories and legends—what do they make of what they 'absorb,' receive, and pay for? What do they do with it?"[8] These practices are not inherently liberatory in the way that some theorists might suggest. These *tactics* are simply ways of constructing alternatives. They are, as de Certeau writes, "victories of the 'weak' over the 'strong,'" or "opportunities that must be seized 'on the wing.'" They manifest themselves in such everyday acts as cooking, dwelling, wandering, and speaking. To cite just one example, he describes what the French call *la perruque*, or "the wig": "*La perruque* is the

7. Ibid., p. 35.

8–11. Michel de Certeau, *The Practice of Everyday Life*, 31, 25, 36, 38–39.

worker's own work disguised as work for his employer. *La perruque* may be as simple a matter as a secretary's writing a love letter on 'company time' or as complex as a cabinetmaker's 'borrowing' a lathe to make a piece of furniture for his living room."[9] These benign appropriations invisibly redirect productivity; they are stolen moments of creativity and freedom, clipped from the cycles of the routine.

In contrast, *strategies* are the techniques of the empowered: "I call a 'strategy' the calculus of force-relationships, which becomes possible when a subject of will and power (a proprietor, an enterprise, a city, a scientific institution) can be isolated from an 'environment.' A strategy assumes a place that can be circumscribed as *proper* (*propre*)"—a word that has many more relevant nuances in French. De Certeau elaborates on this proposition: "The 'proper' is a *triumph of place over time*.... It is also a mastery of places through sight.... It would be legitimate to define the *power of knowledge* by this ability to transform the uncertainties of history into readable spaces."[10]

It is easy to ignore the breadth and sophistication of these assertions if we don't adequately grasp what de Certeau means by "spaces." It is easiest to understand if we start from the premise that space is not something that exists "out there," waiting to be seized, purchased, stolen, or fought over. It is not territory or volume. It does not preexist strategies and practices. Instead, I take de Certeau to mean that we establish all sociospatial entities in a web of force-relationships (this is what Foucault means by *power*) that aspire to appear permanent. Space is becoming, not being. People, institutions, laws, media, and even knowledge identify, claim, define, and circumscribe space to create (the illusion of) being. Space takes on the appearance of an immutable truth through strategies, or the acts of establishing it, shoring it up, naming it, identifying its borders, and maintaining it. Simply put, space does not exist. And we create "place" only through continual acts of seizure. It is the triumph of space over time: "Strategies pin their hopes on the resistance that the *establishment of a place* offers to the erosion of time; tactics on a clever *utilization of time*, of the opportunities it presents and also of the play that it introduces into the foundations of power."[11]

Generally speaking, then, culture is a dialectical process: it is a continual process of freezing and fixing fluid relations (call these strategies); it is
also the reconfiguration or dismantling of those relations through tactics
that tunnel into the bedrock of that power. The objects of design freeze
time. To design is to fix fluid relations. Design seizes space and creates
place. The practice of design, then, exists in the register of strategies. It is
the accumulation of sufficient capital, resources, ingenuity, bandwidth,
media-space, and real estate to claim a certain share of our life. Design is
the process of institutions and corporations imposing places, objects,
visual messages, and ideas into our lives.

While this might sound bleakly critical, it is essential to remember that
science as well as education survive by means of strategies. Moreover, de
Certeau is not shallow; he does not attach venal political and moral values
to his concepts (in other words, it is not the simple case that strategies are
bad and tactics are good). In this way, he is much more the anthropologist
of strategies and tactics, observing and documenting the contested fields of
their deployment. Cultural artifacts—and by association, design artifacts—are always a buttress against time. They are meaningful ways of per-
petuating a set of relations with the goal of sustaining those relations in
fixed positions. But users then adopt those objects, translate those ideas,
and inhabit those spaces in unpredictable, improvisatory ways.

Tactics are, therefore, performative. They are enactments of a given situation or configuration to produce a different end. Performative acts are,
by their very nature, transitory and fleeting. Adopt, adapt, and move on.
By remaking the given, the practices of everyday life rewrite the script and
offer, if only for a moment, novel endings. Writing of urban planning and
design, Barbara Kirshenblatt-Gimblett argues, "Performance is also central
to the production of the urban vernacular, for performance produces spatial form. By performance I mean everything from hanging the laundry
out to hopscotch or lion dancing during the Chinese New Year holiday.
Activities produce distinctive spatial forms, some of which acquire
independent architectural manifestations." To borrow a phrase from de
Certeau, this is cultural poaching. Or as Kirshenblatt-Gimblett puts it,
"This mutation makes the text habitable, like a rented apartment. It

transforms another person's property into a space borrowed for a moment by a transient."[12]

This, in slightly different terms, is the same argument that structuralists like Ferdinand de Saussure and Jacques Lacan made about subjectivity. For these linguistic-based theorists, subjectivity was an aftereffect of the linguistic utterance. Drawing upon that linguistic foundation, de Certeau fashions a similar approach: "In linguistics, 'performance' and 'competence' are different: the act of speaking (with all the enunciative strategies that implies) is not reducible to a knowledge of the language. By adopting the point of view of enunciation—which is the subject of our study—we privilege the act of speaking; according to that point of view, speaking operates within the field of a linguistic system; it effects an appropriation, or reappropriation, of language by its speakers; it establishes a *present* relative to a time and place."[13] If we substitute into de Certeau's formulation terms that are more specific to the design process, we might say that *by adopting the point of view of everyday practices—which is the subject of our study—we privilege the act of consuming; according to that point of view, consuming operates within the field of a design system; it effects an appropriation, or reappropriation, of design by its users; it establishes a present relative to a time and a place.* Frank-Bertholt Raith distills this approach perfectly when he states: "Architecture becomes real only in its performance."[14] That is, the built environment is in a constant state of becoming, or flux. Mitigating this is work that denies its ephemerality and imposes a frozen set of relations upon the world. Power maintains, but everyday practices undermine.

This reformulation underscores the role that time and change play in our everyday encounter with design. It delineates a performative theory of design. It also represents a sensibility that unites a small cluster of designers whose work refuses to foreclose chance, customization, and disintegration, and instead, embraces time's trials and celebrates form's mutability. It acknowledges that the everyday is a constant, quiet practice of appropriation, and it invites that. This work sees form as a process, not an unalterable end, and therefore subverts our expectations of the designer's role by flaunting its formlessness, or at least its disregard of permanent form as the telos of design.

12. Barbara Kirshenblatt-Gimblett, "Performing the City: Reflections on the Urban Vernacular," in *Everyday Urbanism*, eds. John Chase, Margaret Crawford, and John Kaliski (New York: The Monacelli Press, 1999), 19, xxi.

13. Michel de Certeau, *The Practice of Everyday Life*, xiii.

14. Frank-Bertholt Raith, "Everyday Architecture: In What Style Should We Build?" *Daidalos* (issue 75, May 2000): 14.

Finally, why is the ordinary so interesting to us *now*? There are a few reasons. In some cases, it results from the emergence of new technologies of inscription. Embedded sensors, transponders, and processors can now communicate to us mundane information that we had scant access to before. Multiplied by databases and crunched by laptop-sized processors, we can also make better sense of the stream of data that those technologies communicate. The ordinary simply becomes more visible. In other cases, it is amplified by the rise of user-centered design. The emergence of the user and his/her needs as a focus for the design process foregrounds the specificity of daily life, but in a way that must be generalizable. Design offices now deploy user studies and ethnographic methodologies to try to grasp the intimacies of lived experience. This has produced, in some cases, a more humanistic design and a fascination with capturing the quotidian.

Another, perhaps broader, explanation for the rise of work that engages with everyday practices, I would argue, is the suffocating commercialization of all spaces, habits, and experiences. In a brand-saturated culture, those few practices that exist outside of or in confrontation with the heavily sponsored develop a luster of the exotic or real. Where will we find alternatives to a branded life when the battles over ideology are history and the tendrils of free-market capitalism are spreading throughout the world? Are there other stories, are there other ways of designing, that don't simply perpetuate this status quo but instead offer some kind of more meaningful action in our world? We scour the surface of the everyday searching for clues.

Strategies—in de Certeau's sense—exhibit symptoms that appear as the qualities of monumentality, universality, truth, transcendence, and permanence. Ultimately, these attributes seem natural to the designed object. Publicity, awards, curation, and design press combine to perpetuate this fiction of good design as timeless, immutable, or canonical. The real terminus of design work, however, is not so glamorous (and only recently have we begun to take stock of the reality of our consumptive appetites). What distinguishes the work of the loose—mostly Dutch—initiative called do is that it is, instead, engaging more directly with transformability. Rather than pretending that products are permanent, do embraces mutability.

do reincarnate   material: nylon thread, fitting   do creator: Marti Guixé

Death doesn't exist with this "do create" product. The task of *do reincarnate* is to inject fresh life into otherwise tired or over-familiar products. Simply slip the almost invisible thread around your chosen lamp, attach via a light cable, and let it dangle from your ceiling. An old object is suddenly and magically new again as it hangs in midair. *do reincarnate* can be used for more objects: it could be a painting or a photograph. You decide.[15]

15–16. Project descriptions and text that follow can be found on the do Web site, www.dosurf.com.

do has crafted a philosophy and approach to design, consumption, and branding that vaunts its simplicity and parades its trashiness (in the best sense of the word). No-tech style, smudgy graphics, goofy animations, and unflattering photography allow do to carefully shape a low threshold of entry for its audience. It invites participation into its "brand," but what makes that brand a little unusual is that it really barely exists:

do doesn't have any products or services, just a dream. To communicate this dream, do is making all kinds of communication and actions. This way, more people can find out about do. After people know what they can do with do, then products, projects, and services will be added. This is a new way to begin a brand. Usually, a brand starts with a product and then builds a mentality from there . . . *do change* is the name of an experiment from do, a new kind of ever-changing brand which, as the name suggests, depends on what you do.[16]

It is the open nature of do's product "line" that elevates its work beyond a simple slogan or campaign. do is out to mess with the everyday. Its plan is to infect the passive, habitual, and unreflected moments of modern life with antic creativity and polymorphous play. do's self-described goal is to break our addiction to:

soul-destroying habits—ones that slowly but surely drag us down, alter our minds, and make us do bad, bad things. We're not talking about the obvious

65

ones that destroy our health like smoking or drinking or taking drugs or eating mad beef. We're talking about all these comforting, repetitive, second-nature acts we commit every minute of every day: habits we would find most difficult to break if challenged to do so, like that way you always stretch in the morning when you wake up or how you always start reading a magazine from the back page to the front. do change is here to relieve you, to serve you up a big plate of cold turkey to help kick those habits. And all that is required are a few small shocks to your system.[17]

do's materials are conspicuously banal: a T-shirt, tape, nylon string, plywood, or plumbing chain. Delving into the hardware-store vocabulary of our built environment, do's designers insinuate Dadaist reconfigurations that oblige a user to confront the routinization of daily life. Whether it is *do break* (a ceramic vase you can toss but that does not shatter and instead creates a unique crackle pattern) or *do hit* (a cube of steel you beat into a chair with a sledgehammer), each product demands interaction and incites us into a conceptual wrestling match over creativity, originality, consumption, and the mass-production process. With its anonymous style and DIY (do-it-yourself) sensibility—Marcel Duchamp meets Martha Stewart—the do methodology affronts our own passivity. do lowers the barriers to design, and its products command attentive action. By engineering their products with a predisposition for endless reconfiguration and by making that act a traumatic one (throw it, pound it, saw it, scratch it), the designers stare down the "trivial" question of product death. They willingly make us act out the suppressed fury of our consumerist alienation by attacking the products that abet our alienation in the first place. It is as if, to paraphrase William Carlos Williams, the pure products go crazy. Don't like your chair? Smash it with a sledgehammer. Now you have a new chair. What could be more sublime?

This curiously open approach to design and to "products" also infuses the work of Anthony Dunne and Fiona Raby, though in a starkly different way. Their most detailed venture, the *Placebo Project*, investigates the terrain of everyday habit as it intersects technology and collides with design. The project is, ostensibly, a line of electronically augmented furnishings that are conspicuously plain in design. Each contains, however, some material sign of its electronic connection. For *Compass Table*, they inlay an unadorned side table with dozens of compasses. Their plain, straight-backed wooden *Nipple Chair* would pass anonymously except for two small electronic protuberances on the seat back and two discrete ledges for one's feet. These objects serve a dual purpose: to insinuate themselves into the environment through their neutral looks, and to provide a platform for interaction with their electronic program. As Dunne and Raby suggest of their designs, "Made from MDF and usually one other specialist material, the objects are purposely diagrammatic and vaguely familiar. They are open-ended enough to prompt stories but not so open as to bewilder."[18]

Dunne and Raby accept that there is a fuzzy logic to both the human inclination toward technology but also—and this is key—technology's relation to us. As they see it, electronic objects "dream," though they mean this less in a gauzy poetic sense and more in a sober, rational one. Appliances are not brute, dumb, perfect machines: "They leak radiation into the space and objects surrounding them, including our bodies ... electronic objects, it might be imagined, are irrational—or at least they allow their thoughts to wander."[19] This Hertzian, or electromagnetic space, as they term it, is a third space between the user and the object. It dissolves the distinction between us (the people) and them (the machines). It also melts the hard and fast boundaries between public and private, mine and yours: "Lawyers, criminals, and the superstitious are already aware of these issues; designers and architects need to explore them, too."[20] Hertzian space is, to Dunne and Raby, a real space with contours, form, and properties. We must make it "habitable," they believe, because already it is shaping architecture, fashion, infrastructure, law, and behavior: dining rooms in tony restaurants scramble cell phone signals to reduce annoying ringing; materials that block the electromagnetic spectrum are being incorporated into hoods and garments to protect from its mutagenic effects; and people are suing electric companies for damages due to leaking power lines. Between our appliances' incontinent leakages and our own paranoid, superstitious disposition toward machines, there exists this murky, charged realm of failure, imagination, fear, and hope. The inability of

18. Anthony Dunne and Fiona Raby, *Design Noir: The Secret Life of Electronic Objects* (Basel, Boston, Berlin: Birkhauser, 2001), 75.

19–21. Ibid., 8, 26, 8.

design to tap into this reservoir of emotional attachments impoverishes us, Dunne and Raby argue. Design that simply aspires to functional or aesthetic solutions to problems misses this "bizarre world of the 'infra-ordinary,' where stories show that truth is indeed stranger than fiction."[21]

To solicit interaction and affect, Dunne and Raby use design. An indispensable part of their *Placebo Project* are the interviews they publish with their users (who are a hand-picked set of "adopters," or test subjects). This is not strategic user-centered design research, but rather a tactic to explore and experiment with the emotional and psychological relationships that connect people to things. Their *GPS Table*, for example, is a simple, square table with a global positioning sensor built into it. For *GPS* to function correctly, the sensor must establish a signal with a sufficient number of orbiting satellites. When the table is unable to position itself correctly, it indicates this state by displaying the word "lost." Dick, the adopter of the *GPS Table*, describes the uncanny effect this creates:

> **Dunne and Raby:** What kind of theories do you have about when it's lost and when it's found? What do you think is happening?
>
> **Dick:** It's silly really, but because the lights flash, because it moves between its three satellite positions and "lost," it gives it a sense of being alive. There's no other word for it. . . . You get the sense that you have to say, "Is it all right?" It's silly to talk about treating it as a sort of person, but it is – "I'd better go and check to see if the table's there." [22]

Ultimately, they don't envision manufacturers producing their designs. Instead, their projects belong to the realm of critical design practice. They engage a darker world, one they call Design Noir, in which the relationships between products and the people who use them are not always so shiny, happy, and neat. Instead, their work taps into a messier emotional landscape of fear, pain, erotic attachment, and loneliness.

Dunne and Raby approach this realm by designing objects that really don't play the games of form, fashion, or even functionality. They engineer their projects as openings for experiences, stories, and relationships. The point of the *Placebo Project* is to explore everyday life, to "illustrate the

22–24. Ibid., no page listed, 6, 7.

narrative space entered by using and misusing a simple electronic product, [and show] how interaction with everyday electronic technologies can generate rich narratives that challenge the conformity of everyday life by short-circuiting our emotions and states of mind. These stories blend the physical reality of place with electronically mediated experience and mental affect. They form part of the pathology of material culture."[23] Their projects, then, spark conversation. Obsession over the form of the objects is practically superfluous to the goal, which is to generate narratives. The "design" is not located solely within the furnishings they produce. To insist on the primariness of the designed artifact is to miss totally their mission. Their product is instead some peculiar combination of the furniture, its physical and electronic affordances, the people they pick, the interviews, and the record of it all. As with do or Marti Guixé's work, the style of the object is minimally important at best, and sometimes barely relevant. It is sufficient to design it enough to make it suit the job—to blend in. The real action is in the cultural strings it pulls or, to put it into Dunne and Raby's terms, in how it supports us in "customizing reality."[24]

To explore the formlessness of design is not necessarily to forgo form altogether, which would be impossible. Everything perceptible has some form to it. What distinguishes this approach is the abandonment of form as the first principle for design success. Instead, designers are venturing into the muddier regions of design's impact on our social life. They are exploring alternative ways of using the process to address social, emotional, and political ends. Again, the transformation of the social environment—not just the built environment—emerges as the focal point of the project.

For example, in their *Fences and Doors* project for Droog Design, NEXT Architects abandons the traditional role of designers—to create something new—in favor of a simple reconfiguration of the existing. They slightly alter the standard wooden fence, for instance, creating fleeting opportunities for social encounters. In one case, they provide the outlines of gardening tools in the fence itself by perforating the material, creating slots for storing tools that are accessible to residents on both sides. In another, extensions on each side of the fence serve as surfaces for table tennis. Folded up, the fence retains its iconic status as a brutal barrier. Folded down, it allows for a friendly match between neighbors. Their goal, as is evident through the clarity of their design, is to override the fence's tendency to separate us. Clear enough. What distinguishes their work is its goofy simplicity. They assail this icon — the symbol of social alienation and dysfunction in our privatopias — through humor, not heavy-handed social messages. That, of course, is the gamble that their project takes. It can be seen as overbearing, or forced social interaction: design as bad, centralized, friendship engineering. This risk is not unique to their work. Any project that asks its users to participate in it, collaborate with it, or innervate it risks that. It also must come to terms with venturing into a consumer landscape of social passivity and engineered complaisance. But this is a pernicious stereotype of consumption. As de Certeau points out, people are always transforming the given to their own ends. We are careless to think otherwise.

Design and the everyday are inextricably intertwined. Because it plays such a constitutive role in everyday life, it is hard to say that there is design work that truly engages, or does not engage, the everyday. When we pull out our Philippe Starck potty in the middle of the night for a wayward toddler, what could be more everyday? This is, I believe, Lefebvre's point. The ordinary is ungraspable, slippery, and constantly confounding. Nothing is easier to point to and yet nothing eludes analysis more immediately. It is conceptual quicksilver.

But this does not therefore lead to a conclusion that the everyday is irrelevant to a critical understanding of design practice. The ordinary and the extraordinary are not absolutes, but a continuum, just as tactics and strategies are bound together in a messy, sometimes indeterminate grasp. But there is work that assumes a different posture relative to design orthodoxy. And there are qualities common to these projects, even if their differences are sometimes more stark. The great irony, of course, is that few fields possess a shorter memory than product design. Its products disappear from our lives in the blink of an eye and with little ceremony. Product design is like the fast food of our built environment. It fills us up with dubious calories and then we come right back for more, with scant awareness of what we just consumed. While often aspiring to transcend the present, most design gets ingloriously dragged away by fashion's cruel undertow.

The everyday is corrosive. To consume is to absorb completely but also to waste away and destroy. Time wins out. Always. What is refreshing about work like that considered here is that it does not fight that current but flows downstream with it, affirming the passing of fads, the perversity of fashion, and the righteousness of decay. Flow, flux, fluidity — these are the most powerful qualities of everyday life. By evading fixed form, such work opens a productive dialogue with the user, prompting uncontrollable acts of creativity and disfiguration. It is wise to the tactical habits of the everyday. We may consume everyday, but eventually, the everyday consumes us.

Jamer Hunt teaches at the University of the Arts in Philadelphia, where he is Director of the Master's Program in Industrial Design, a graduate laboratory for postindustrial design. He holds a doctorate in cultural anthropology, has served on the Board of Directors of the American Center for Design, and has consulted and worked at design practices such as Smart Design inc., frogdesign, and Virtual Beauty. His own work explores the poetics and politics of the built environment.

JONATHAN BELL
RUINS, RECYCLING, SMART BUILDINGS, AND THE ENDLESSLY
TRANSFORMABLE ENVIRONMENT

There is strong public awareness of the role of design in shaping and selling a product. Bombarded by brands, messages, logos, and exhortations, the everyday life of the consumer is augmented by constantly refreshed sets of media-created standards. "Design" has become a value-added extra, a magical component that can be sprinkled like fairy dust onto a project to align it with the right market segment, while marketing budgets are devoted to "educating" consumers about design, highlighting an unbreakable bond between the product, lifestyle, and any useful historical associations that might be made between today's product and memorable past glories or values. More often than not, a product's "life cycle"—that is to say the cradle-to-grave trajectory taken by an object from fabrication, through marketing, consumption, use, rejection, and eventual destruction, as opposed to the concept of "life span," which only refers to the third and fourth of these stages—is defined not by its physical but social and technological durability. Both of these factors are mediated by forces far beyond the consumer's control.

Perhaps we need to think in terms of life cycle rather than life span, raising manufacturer and consumer awareness of the secret life of objects, composed from their various interactions. How might we enhance the value of life cycle in product design, stressing sustainability over culturally dependent factors like fashion and lifestyle? What role does technology play in defining life cycle, and how do we compare product with architectural life cycle? It has been suggested that the economic and social forces shaping architecture, particularly in the domestic realm, have created a very different definition of life cycle, one that places an emphasis on re-use and flexibility. Product design—the realm of the object—must respond in kind. Perhaps most importantly, how does the "everyday," that fluid definition of our material culture, fit into "design"? What of the existence of "strangely familiar" objects—those products and things that arise from the constant interpretation of the everyday by design, media, and creative culture? This is a new frontier for designers, a realm where conventional definitions of functions and intentions are blurred. Will the strangely familiar object reinterpret our relationship with consumption?

Public awareness of and desire for design comes at a high price: it threatens to overwhelm the cultural value of the everyday object and environment. Simple sociological analysis would suggest that the desire and expectation created by advertising ensures that reality invariably fails to match up. We don't live in a world of Gap-ad perfection, a Pottery Barn or IKEA catalogue-styled environment where nothing is out of place and everything is in harmony. Anticonsumerist activists have highlighted the futility of trying to match these impossible levels of perfection, yet we are collectively conditioned to struggle onward, however much we acknowledge (often ironically) that we are chasing a dream.

We are constantly assaulted by fresh definitions of the new, with the everyday a vital part of the feedback loop that defines our media-driven culture; it is rapidly dismissed as outdated, due for an upgrade or an overhaul. The everyday is also considered home of the "authentic," the culturally unsullied: an experience or product that remains "pure." Oxymoronically, the authentic exists only to be deauthenticated by association, as it is subsumed for the purpose of advertising. The worlds of fashion photography, rock music, fine art, cooking, even interior design, could all be said to be engaged in a constant quest for a new authenticity. To discard the everyday is aspirational, a symbol of progress and transformation.

In this environment, a product's life cycle becomes almost irrelevant: how many objects are we encouraged to use until obsolescence? While the rise of consumer groups in the postwar period (the Consumers' Association in the United Kingdom, the Consumers' Union in the United States[1]) has largely overcome the pernicious problem of "planned obsolescence" in terms of physical quality, very little can be done to overcome technical and social obsolescence. How many times have you replaced, as opposed to upgraded, your personal computer in the past decade? Chances are that replacements outnumber upgrades, as the modular design of the personal computer was overtaken by the social and cultural obsolescence created by software engineers, game developers, and our own desire for more that is new. Products have been reduced to transient objects that reflect fads and fashions rather than actual needs and demands. Yet can this model of production and consumption continue to provide a satisfactory experience? There are those—scientists, environmentalists, politicians—who believe it can't, and stress the need for less overt consumption and more emphasis on extending life cycle. Can sustainability be integrated into a system that places such importance on the link between progress and consumption?

Combining Longevity with Lifestyle

There are many ways to extend a product's life cycle. The exhibition *Strangely Familiar* illustrates a range of objects and environments with "secret lives," transcending the pervasive systems that drive and sustain consumer culture. To give just one example, Anthony Dunne and Fiona Raby address the ubiquity of electronic gadgetry in our lives and the uses to which it is put in their book *Design Noir*. With this concept, they attempt to undermine the things we take for granted by adding a new spin to the familiar. Likening the contemporary state of product design to the Hollywood blockbuster, with its attendant superstars, studio system, promotional outlets, and public expectations, the pair consider Design Noir to be its antithesis, focusing on ways that the "psychological dimensions of experiences offered through electronic products can be expanded,"[2] just as the thoughtful indie film hopefully delves deeper into its characters than

1. The former was founded by Lord Young of Dartington in 1957, the latter in America in 1936.

2. Anthony Dunne and Fiona Raby, *Design Noir: The Secret Life of Electronic Objects* (Basel, Boston, Berlin: Birkhauser, 2001).

the surface-skimming studio picture. Best of all, the duo surmises, are the products that completely escape the attention of designers by transgressing their accepted function through an added layer of uncertainty. For example, their "truth phone" contains an integrated lie detector of the type sold at specialist surveillance shops. A telephone call therefore becomes a battle of wits, with technology intervening and perhaps overriding cultural and social clues as to the nature of a conversation.

Dunne and Raby's objects are all about engaging in fresh dialogues with established uses, transferring technology into new contexts. In the case of Design Noir, it is the designer who reinterprets that which already exists. The vast majority of transgressively used products are not pre-planned: they develop after the product has been consumed. Rarely, however, does the transgression remain in the consumer's rather than the producer's control. A prime example has been the rise of the SMS (Short Messages Service). Europe's GSM (Global System for Mobile Communications) phone network included the ability to transmit short, one hundred sixty-character messages from phone to phone, a feature added almost as a technological afterthought. Largely driven by the youth market rather than the predicted business market, SMS use spread rapidly, accelerating by fourteen hundred percent in 2000 with billions of messages sent each year. SMS messaging is now considered a key reason for owning and using a mobile phone. Service providers produce glossy advertisements extolling various scenarios for its use—flirting, socializing, even foreplay—swiftly corralling what was once subversive back into the mainstream.

These examples each credit the designer with initiating the transgression, suggesting that the principle way in which life cycle can be extended is through relying on the existing system of designer, manufacturer, and consumer. If, as already discussed, a product's life cycle bears very little relationship to its actual degradation and decay through use, then transgression—hacking, customizing, music sampling—is one way in which life cycle can be extended and brought closer to the true desires and demands of the consumer. One only has to look at specialist interests and hobbies to see that myriad interest groups cater to their own needs through the adaptation of existing products. The rise of file-sharing utilities on the Internet such as Napster, WinMX, KaZaA, and Audiogalaxy is another example of transgressive products. File-sharing, software developed to exploit the Internet's core functions, which created an almost unbreakable network for trading large files, proved far more difficult to reintegrate into existing structures of music marketing and delivery, even though several companies tried. The practice was deemed to be a sufficient threat to the music industry, meaning that the only alternative was to legislate against them. Napster officially folded in September 2002, its life cycle curtailed by its opposition to existing systems. Any resurrection will be in a guise far removed from its subversive beginnings.

Life cycle, then, is an artificially created construct that runs counter to common sense and our everyday experience in favor of stimulating a perpetually expanding cycle of production and consumption. As we have seen, although a product's life cycle can be extended and developed to suit one's own means, the consumer's everyday attempts at generating authenticity are constantly under assault from the producers' desire to manufacture authenticity of their own. Hence we have "cool hunters," corporate-sponsored seekers of new developments at "street level," hoping to co-opt the authentic into the mass market. Producers might wish to ensure that a product's life cycle is artificially sustained, at least until a more profitable product comes along. This is the business model that drives the technology industry. The computer games console is built and sold at a loss: the games will make the profit in the long run. This places the console's life cycle at the whim of the producer, who can decide when to stop the supply of games and switch consumer allegiance to another console, for example. Cultural production, in the form of media, can be endlessly recycled and resold in different shapes, forms, and formats and we are urged to upgrade and move on, trading up our video disc, laser disc, Betamax player, VHS player, DVD player, DVD recorder, etc., etc. The next generation always promises to be faster, more efficient, and better in every way.

Is it in producers' interests to consider life cycle more carefully? All the evidence seems to suggest that this is not the case, and it is only where legislative issues force their hands that companies have paid more attention to the importance of a product's extended life cycle. Otherwise, the emphasis remains on more, not less. The strangely familiar object is discouraged. Although a somewhat marginalized area of the market, sustainable design has made enormous inroads into changing the way life cycle is perceived. Sustainable design seeks to produce responsible objects by understanding that a product might not last forever and therefore needs to be easily recycled into other products with other uses, or that a product could have an almost infinite life span and should therefore be simple to build and service, while having the least possible environmental impact. How can the tenets of sustainable design be applied to product design and architecture to address the negative connotations of truncated product life cycles and the relentless emphasis on the new?

The Self-Inflicted Shock of the New

Perhaps the first task is to address the association between novelty and progress. Early modernist imagery was dominated by futuristic urban visions: cities of tomorrow that broke completely with the past. In part, this relentless newness was an acknowledgment that there could be nothing romantic about a modernist ruin. The idylls of imagined decay that pervade classical architecture, making every building a potentially verdant mass of crumbling columns, pediments, and abandoned caryatids, had no place in the modernist canon. Soanian vaults lent themselves well to imagined decay, as attested by visionary artist Joseph Michael Gandy's stylized view of the architect's Bank of England (1788–1833) as it might appear many centuries in the future. Even Albert Speer, Hitler's architect, believed himself to be designing for a thousand-year Reich, followed by a few more millennia of ruined triumphalism thanks to the overscaled monuments he proposed for Berlin. In stark contrast, modernism proposed glistening cities of glass, steel, and concrete. Le Corbusier's *La Ville Radieuse* called for the demolition of huge swaths of ancient Paris, an idea that is today as laughable as it is unthinkable. Yet sweeping changes were made, due to the speed at which society came to depend on transportation, information, and communications technology. Otherwise, technology was crudely inserted into the urban fabric, with planning and architecture secondary to the needs of transport and communications. As a foretaste of what was to come, trees in 1920s New York were removed from sidewalks because they were deemed hazardous obstacles for the newfangled automobiles beginning to clog the streets.

3. Reyner Banham, *Megastructure: Urban Futures of the Recent Past* (London: Thames & Hudson, 1976).

Modernism's transparent desire to restructure society was evident in the ultimate architectural device: the megastructure. Not simply the insertion of new infrastructure on top of the old city but the desire to re-create it entirely, the megastructure was a building that grew to epic proportions, connected only to other megastructures. Reyner Banham, among others, catalogued the origins of the megastructural ideal[3] with many unbuilt conceptual projects and few existing examples, but even the backwards-looking subtitle of his book, *Urban Futures of the Recent Past*, acknowledged that the megastructural concept was doomed to failure. Its principle legacy was for single-use developments such as the mall, where it remains the dominant building form (and confirms its isolation by being an inward-centric building, rather than open to and embracing its surroundings).

The flaws of modernism as an all-encompassing ideal only emphasized the strangely familiar in architecture and urbanism. Our antipathy toward modernism's candid adoration of the new is confirmed by our experience of contemporary cities that have had the misfortune to find themselves destroyed or abandoned. Sarajevo, Beirut, Chernobyl: all appear more or less intact from the air, with the grids of their ice-tray, punch-card architecture giving few clues to the devastation within. These are tragic failures of diplomacy, science, and progress with little or no redeeming romanticism, their life cycle tied solely to their ability to function. Modernism's failures are perhaps best encapsulated by a single, iconic ruin—architect-critic Charles Jencks' favorite bogeyman, Minoru Yamasaki's ill-fated high-rise public-housing project, Pruitt Igoe—a symbol of catastrophic single-mindedness.

This one-track-minded pursuit of an architecture of technological determinism peaked with the high period of the International Style, when the global dominance of functionalism coincided with the start of the widespread introduction of mainframe computers. Here was an architecture of rigid functionalism, ostensibly flexible yet ultimately tailored to the hierarchy of the workplace. Twentieth-century office design provides a good opportunity to study the role of life cycle in architecture, as furniture and fittings gradually migrated from integral architectural components to free-standing, infinitely configurable elements that mirror our changing work patterns.[4] The Steelcase Q, perhaps the ultimate embodiment of the mobile workstation, was a 1997 concept from designers at IDEO that was actually self-powered, designed to trundle around the empty wastelands of open space—perhaps in search of other Steelcase Qs with which to share information, partner up, and graze. The new flexibility has seen a corresponding increase in building life cycle; today, we are used to tech companies in old buildings, retrofitted for high-speed communications and networking.

Scrappy bits of old technology continue to lurk in the urban environment, whether large (the High Line in New York, the abandoned rail line that runs on elevated tracks through West Chelsea and might one day become a public park[5]) or small (the Rabbit service offered in the U.K. in the late 1980s was an early mobile phone provider that allowed you to make calls within one hundred meters of a transmitter, the location of which was indicated by an inverted "R" sign. A few of these signs still exist, reminders of a once-innovative service obliterated by technological advances). Retrofitting our cities to accommodate new demands might not be the most elegant solution, but new and old can coexist, sometimes happily, sometimes not. With conservation and reuse swiftly becoming central tenets of urban planning, the modernist desire for a clean slate has been subsumed by the need for preservation. To address, integrate, and complement the past has become a fundamental architectural requirement. Cities must flex, not buckle.

The city is composed not only of myriad interlocking, interrelated spaces, but also multiple experiences and interpretations. Modernism's dismal record at creating inspirational planning lies in part in the movement's refusal to recognize the city as a whole: the modernist city planner's vision versus the everyday experience of the resident on the ground. Rather than see the city as a stage set or an empty theater awaiting its actors, it is better to consider it a play in progress. This theory was extolled by philosopher Henri Lefebvre, who conceived of the city as social space, with

4. *On the Job: Design and the American Office*, ed. Donald Albrecht and Chrysanthe B. Broikos (New York: Princeton Architectural Press, 2000).

5. See www.thehighline.org/.

6. Kenneth Powell,
*Architecture Reborn:
The Conversion and
Reconstruction of Old
Buildings* (London:
Laurence King
Publishing, 1999).

production informed by power structures and the interaction between public/private areas. We now know that our cities are capable of reorganizing themselves to accommodate vast amounts of change, rather than having change foisted upon them in the form of wholesale demolition and rebuilding. Conservation need not be the enemy of progress.

Unlike product design, architects have a far greater incentive to extend the life cycle of their "product." In London, the Georgian terraced houses constructed by the thousands in the eighteenth and nineteenth centuries were originally intended as speculative ventures, a cheaply built commodity constructed as a money-making venture by landowners and builders to capitalize on their property holdings. By the postwar era, vast tracts of Georgian housing lay derelict, a century past their expected life span and architecturally unfashionable. Despite a great deal of demolition—often to make way for modernist developments—conservation groups began to spring up, disturbed by the seemingly needless destruction of usable building stock as well as the street pattern and urban fabric these carefully planned developments had created. Today, the Georgian townhouse is among the most prized form of domicile in England, an architectural status symbol. The combination of quality and space, plus the prestige conferred by age and extensive period features, has made these homes desirable. They have become adaptable by default to use and abuse (conversion to industrial units and apartments, for example), so their life cycle has proved almost infinitely extendable, thanks to economic conditions that cast these survivors in a different light.

The contemporary city is fragmented and confusing—retrofitted to accommodate new technologies, rather than be replaced on a wholesale basis, creating a series of parallel life cycles that add up to a cohesive whole. In architecture and urban design, life cycle and economics have become closely linked, although there are still huge discrepancies. Kenneth Powell, in the introduction to his book *Architecture Reborn,*[6] points out that not only are there vast disparities in the treatment of old buildings between East and West, old world and new, but also that the ostensibly similar architectural cultures of modernism in, for example, the United

Kingdom and the United States, each value their built heritage in an entirely different way.

As architectural life cycle has extended, the past two decades have seen a shift in the perception of architecture, in particular the way in which the arrangement and configuration of domestic space has become a totem of lifestyle. Housing that can accommodate fluctuating desires and activities, transformable architecture that flatters us with the possibility of a life of change and excitement, was born out of the loft boom. Loft and warehouse spaces were themselves by-products of shifts in production and consumption patterns—the need to ship goods by sea and rail, with the associated storage and warehousing at the heart of major metropolitan centers, was superseded by road hauling, refrigerated storage, and more efficient delivery methods. Warehouses became surplus to the economic function of the city, existing in marginal zones that were no longer considered to be prime real estate.

Sharon Zukin's *Loft Living* (1982) was one of the first books to identify the trend and study the loft phenomenon. Today, such books number in the hundreds, glossy coffee-table tomes that have less to do with the reappropriation of real estate than the selling of a lifestyle. As physical space became more expensive, the initial wave of loft owners—traditionally those with a creative background who could both live and work in the unencumbered space and were unfazed by the lack of economic activity normally associated with residential areas (shops, transportation, restaurants)—were replaced. The loft "lifestyle" became associated with new money, and a premium was attached to inner-city space. Loft sizes shrank, and developers spread their net further, preserving the open-plan approach to the division of living area, yet drastically reducing the amount of square footage available. The three- to five-thousand-square-foot loft could just as easily become four, five, or six smaller units, offering far greater financial return. City dwellers were presented with the oxymoron of the newly built loft, a shell building that mimicked the scale and flexibility of the original industrial space but was designed from the outset for domestic use.

Now that the compressed urban fabric is finally stripped of all empty buildings, the only available option is to subdivide again and again. Multifunctional spaces are a response. Loft living transcended conventional domesticity, a strangely familiar lifestyle that subverted the original use for economic and social reasons. Numerous practices have gone further by proposing transformable environments that can attach themselves, podlike, to existing structures to change their function. Reducing the needs of a building's occupants down to a series of modular structures equates architecture with product design, a designation it has traditionally shied away from. However much modernist theorists and proponents admired the technical and physical efficiencies of the production line, architecture remained sociologically wedded to its role as supplier of one-off or custom solutions.

As with product design, architectural subversion has traditionally been swiftly accommodated into the mainstream. The protoindustrial aesthetic favored by architects from the very start of the modern movement took existing technologies and transferred them to the architectural realm. Le Corbusier's "machine for living in" arose from the architect's fascination with mass production and the forms of the machine age, unsullied by ornament in the search for efficiency. Today, we might dismiss this as an unattainable ideal at odds with our individual idiosyncrasies, but the need to make buildings more efficient is unabated. Multifunctionality, portability, and prefabrication remain closely integrated concepts, perhaps because of their dependence on manufacturing rather than craft origins. The portable house in particular is a recurrent device in utopian architectural debate, as is architecture that adapts materials and products to domestic use. Yet although the utopian prototypes for mass-market housing developed by architects like Albert Frey, Paul Rudolph, and Buckminster Fuller, and those for the Case Study Houses took the International Style and humanized it through a reduction in scale, the populist image of the mass-produced house was strictly retrogressive. The promise behind Levittown and its many imitators was not of a crisp-edged futurism, but of a folksy evocation of a suburban idyll, with modernism conferring speed, efficiency, and affordability on the whole enterprise.

Contemporary architects have to work with these spectres of modernist failure and visual conservatism. Despite this, a movement is emerging that extends function as it melds product with space. Shigeru Ban's paper-tube structures take a material best associated with impermanence and transform it into shelter, while Sean Godsell's shipping-container house takes a standard industrial product and moves it into the architectural realm. The *Technological Cabins* constructed by Wes Jones Partners use a similar principle: transportable space. LOT-EK, which also works with shipping containers and other premanufactured and converted items, uses its work to extend both the life cycle of the object and the host structure: strangely familiar, indeed. Architects whose work focuses on the transformable, including but by no means limited to Steven Holl in New York, Mark Guard in London, and Stephen Varaday in Australia,[7] use mostly conventional materials to create adaptable environments. These works are essentially a continuation of the modernist tradition (like Rietveld's compact arrangement of ever-changing space in the Schroder House), while managing to eschew its traditional intolerance of the old. Walls, doors, and partitions slide and fold, function is hidden until needed. Guard's 1997 project for a prototypical "transformable apartment" showed how the inner-city loft could be structured to form a one-, two-, or no-bed apartment, a space dedicated to the changing needs of its users.

Could the life cycle demands of architecture be applied to product design? An adaptable architecture is not a radical proposal. Regardless of the problems posed by initial design, a building can be reconfigured, whether it's an open-plan warehouse or a speculatively built Georgian terrace: the organic pattern of the city accommodates this kind of change far better than wholesale reconstruction. In societies where purchasing a property outright is acknowledged as a goal, the huge investment in one's own home means that the desire to adapt and accommodate changing needs has become a central tenet of domesticity. Stewart Brand's *How Buildings Learn*[8] traced ways that small-scale alterations add up to create a cohesive whole, ensuring the continued survival of streetscape and urban environment provided that buildings are constructed in such a way as to facilitate constant adaptation. Homeowners have known for decades that

7. The Transformable House, eds. Jonathan Bell and Sally Godwin (*Architectural Design*, vol. 70, no. 4, 2000).

8. Stewart Brand, How Buildings Learn: What Happens After They're Built (New York: Viking, 1994).

the house is an adaptive mechanism, raw material for almost infinite functional and stylistic combinations. The postwar surge in the do-it-yourself craze has evolved into a global industry worth billions of dollars, as homeowners are encouraged to adapt and extend the life cycle of their properties. Do-it-yourself, while providing a fertile ground for commentators and students of changing social mores in taste, furnishings, and domestic arrangements, tends to be frowned upon by the architectural establishment. Despite this, numerous architects have evolved an aesthetic that melds the everyday with architecture's traditional "high art" approach, creating an aesthetic that simultaneously retains the memory of the past and the authentic while progressing with a cultural agenda.

Frank Gehry's house in Santa Monica, California (started 1978) was perhaps the first domestic space to address this gray area of design. It was deconstruction personified, an architectural object from a high-cultural tradition that took the language and material of so-called "low" culture—the tract house, backyard, cheap warehouse, and chain-linked lot—and used them to acknowledge the continual transformation of the average domestic space, peeling back structure and creating new forms and juxtapositions in the process. Others have followed. Doug Garofalo's *Markow Residence* in Prospect Heights, Illinois, is a similar exploration of the role of space, material, and dynamism in the typical suburban tract, exploding convention with a plan that plays with perspective and scale. The early work of Rem Koolhaas' Studio OMA also fetishized the role of everyday materials. In his *Villa d'All Ava* in Saint-Cloud, Paris (1984–1991) Koolhaas reuses raw industrial barrier material for its roof terracing, in bright orange, rejecting any notion of an imposed modernist order.

Such architecture neatly addresses the dominant paradox of our era—that consumers expect things to be simultaneously new and capable of remembering. In product design, this has given rise to retro styling, fast becoming the prevalent mode of expression as designers and producers seek to revive elements of iconic products for a new market segment. Retro design is an acknowledged tactic for those seeking to address their "heritage" or brand history. The auto industry is perhaps the most visible advocate of so-called "heritage mining," where the strangely familiar forms of the past are not so much teased from our memories as presented for us in their entirety. The first, highly visible phase of retro design—the new MINI Cooper, VW Beetle, Ford GT40, Lincoln Continental Concept—is gradually being replaced by a more considered approach.

Extending the Cycle

Can we reconcile our desire for permanence in the places we live and the things that we buy with the even stronger desire for progress? Disposability isn't necessarily the enemy—despite its connotations of material waste and prolificacy, the disposable camera is one of the most efficient recycling systems in existence. Arguably, all objects become multifunctional once their recyclability is taken for granted. The beauty of a system that allows for an open life-cycle loop is that the second, third, fourth use is almost infinite, limited only by our imaginations. Traditionally, designs that exploit their recycled status for aesthetic or economic effect, such as Victor Papanek's celebrated "world bottle" project,[9] have been marginalized and kept away from the cultural mainstream. The explicitly recycled object remains something of an anomaly, an art object, rather than an extension of the everyday, although this is not for want of trying. Designer Jane Atfield's recycled chairs typify this approach. Atfield used high-density polythene recycled from household bottles to make the *RCP2 Chair* (1995). While its form is simple and unpretentious, the object draws its resonance from the signs of its former life, the colored flecks of plastic items used in the basic, raw recycling process.[10] Atfield's chairs and Papanek's proposed bottle are strangely familiar objects, recycled products that make a virtue of their secondhand nature, encouraging us to identify and revisit their former incarnations, yet neither succeeded in bringing their particular extensions of life cycle to a mass market.

Addressing waste and material use needs to be a key element of product design. The sheer amount of waste generated creates whole cityscapes of rubbish, with parts of the globe dedicated to sieving through the detritus to recover material just so that it can reenter the cycle. In the past forty years, the average American's waste production has doubled, with a weekly output of 14.3 kilograms, the highest in the world.[11] Whole cultures are

9. Noting that food and drink containers were often integrated into vernacular structures as building materials in developing countries, Papanek proposed a stackable, interlocking bottle, a ready-made building block that could be used to construct buildings cheaply and simply, conferring a secondary, more important function on a mass-produced object. Victor Papanek, *Design for the Real World* (New York: Random House, 1971).

10. Atfield's work was featured in the exhibition *Transformations: The Art of Recycling*, which ran from March 25, 2000, through September 8, 2002, at the Pitt Rivers Museum, Oxford, England. The exhibition displayed the work of Zürich-based design group Freitag, including their messenger bag constructed from truck tarpaulins (1999).

11. "Disposable Planet?" report, news.bbc.co.uk/hi/english/static/in_depth/world/1001/disposable_planet, 2002.

12. See
www.photovoyage
.auroaquanta.com/pv/
recycle; photographer
Jose Azel.

13. John Tierney,
"Recycling Is
Garbage," originally
published in the *New
York Times Magazine*,
June 30, 1996.

14. On July 1, 2002,
glass and plastic
recycling was stopped
for two years and
one year respectively,
under proposals
introduced by Mayor
Michael Bloomberg.
Source: Natural
Resources
Defense Council,
www.nrdc.org.

15. William
McDonough and
Michael Braungart,
*Cradle to Cradle:
Rethinking the Way
We Make Things*
(San Francisco: North
Point Press, 2002).

adapting to a world of rubbish—such as the villages in Guangdong, China, that are dedicated to high-tech recycling, a highly hazardous industry that uses child labor to sift through the debris of the computer age— our industrial age—with its great tangles of wires, dumpsters full of deadly PCBs, cases constructed from all-too-durable shatterproof ABS plastic, and assorted digital detritus. Currently, just over twenty-eight percent of America's waste (some 220 million tons a year) is recycled:[12] the alternative—landfills—are cheap and plentiful in comparison. However, with European Union legislation demanding that landfill dumping be cut by two-thirds by 2015, the onus is on designers and manufacturers to find ways to reduce the need for waste disposal and increase recyclability.

Despite the very visible manifestations of a materials crisis, recycling continues to get a bad press.[13] With landfill sites, in America at least, in no danger of overflowing, a city like New York could still confidently cancel recycling schemes, citing (understandable) monetary concerns.[14] A new wave of postenvironmentalist thinking is also taking the fundamental principles of the movement and reinterpreting them. In the book *Cradle to Cradle*,[15] William McDonough and Michael Braungart propose that the environmental movement—and sustainability in general—is out of step with the demands of contemporary consumers, offering them "depressing" connotations: a hair-shirted life of repentance for their former profligate ways. Instead, the authors suggest an alternative approach, one that considers a product's life cycle from the outset (rebranding "sustainable design" as "smart design" in the process). Describing the current "cradle to grave" product life cycle as uneconomic, especially when natural resources are replaced with toxic by-products in the manufacture, use, and disposal of objects, they propose a "cradle to cradle" system whereby industry and production is geared to generating positive by-products. In the process, recycling is dismissed as a "feel-good program" with little economic viability, thanks to the way in which materials are treated before being integrated into products: hard to extract, and almost worthless for reuse in their original form.

Even paper lasts considerably longer than one might imagine—dig deep into the strata of the modern landfill and you'll find newspapers dating back decades, perfectly preserved. In June 2002, British media reacted with outrage to the news that there was a fast-growing "fridge mountain"—a million discarded refrigerators and chiller cabinets—mounting up in landfill sites around the country, awaiting the construction of a specialist plant to remove toxic CFCs from their plumbing before they could be recycled. The fridge mountain was a monument not to rampant consumerism or conspicuous excess, still less an indicator of a constant quest for betterment, but simply an indication of how easily bureaucracy and organization can fail the best intentions. Traditionally, old appliances were returned to stores, which then shipped them to developing countries for a second life. While this practice might seem to be usefully prolonging the life of a product, it was damaging rather than productive. As well as taking shipping into account, the developing countries would be lumbered with inefficient, polluting devices with even less chance of having the expensive facilities for stripping down the appliances once they finally failed, putting the country at risk from the pollutants shipped so generously from the developed country.

Contemporary recycling works best on a less overt level, when industrial processes learn to integrate their waste cycle into the economic model that drives production, rather than treat waste as a natural by-product. Just as we have come to appreciate that buildings are not necessarily transient and can be adapted to our present-day demands, will the developed world come to a similar understanding with objects, as the strangely familiar comes to dominate our object-centric consumption? Just as modernism ultimately diversified to celebrate the banal and everyday—the rough textures of architectural Brutalism,[16] or the everyday cues of Robert Venturi's early postmodernism—so we now recognize the value of the urban fabric as a whole.

Conclusion

We now have a more humane modern architecture that emphasizes rather than denies the relationship between old and new. But the ramifications of a society better attuned to historical, social, ecological, and aesthetic considerations goes further. As many of the projects in the exhibition

16. Alison and Peter Smithson's Secondary School in Hunstanton, England (1951–1954), with its exposed plumbing, strict structural and material honesty, and simple, unpretentious form-making, is generally held to be the first New Brutalist building, although the term later became associated almost exclusively with architecture that used raw, exposed concrete—Le Corbusier's *beton brut*.

Strangely Familiar demonstrate, elements of contemporary architecture are increasingly resembling product design, while a related strand of product design is working to subvert traditional cultural meanings and functions. Perhaps consumers are entering a phase of enhanced awareness of the possibilities and histories of the object, the role—and importance—of the recycled, reused, and extended life cycle. The crossovers between product and environment, use and reuse, are increasingly at the heart of our urban experience. We are learning to acknowledge the city as a constantly recycled collection of spaces, form, and content that can be reinterpreted and reevaluated without being slavishly imitated or ruthlessly dispatched. The socially and culturally responsible architecture and design of the future will draw upon this continuously refreshed history, a strange, almost subconscious familiarity with the city—past, present, and future.

Jonathan Bell is a writer and freelance journalist. He was the editor of *Carchitecture* (United Kingdom: August Birkhäuser, August 2001) and the coeditor (with Sally Godwin) of "The Transformable House" (*Architectural Design*, 2000). He writes regularly for *Blueprint*, *Wallpaper**, and *Graphics International*, and is also the coeditor of *things*, a journal about objects and their histories. Bell lives in London.

RITUALS OF USE

DUNNE & RABY

**COMPASS TABLE, ELECTRICITY DRAIN, ELECTRO-DRAUGHT
EXCLUDER, GPS TABLE, LOFT, NIPPLE CHAIR, PARASITE LIGHT,
AND PHONE TABLE FROM PLACEBO PROJECT, 2001**

The eight objects that comprise *Placebo Project* were created to investigate people's attitudes, experiences, and relationships to electromagnetic fields, particularly those emitted by electronic consumer goods. Anthony Dunne and Fiona Raby solicited individuals to "adopt" one of the objects and to live with it for a brief period of time. They documented and interviewed these people as part of the project. Purposefully straightforward in their appearance, each object has been outfitted with some material or technology that will perform or behave in certain ways. Some reveal the presence of invisible electromagnetic radiation, such as *Compass Table*, which contains twenty-five magnetic compasses that spin when electronic products such as a laptop computer are placed on it, or *Nipple Chair*, which includes a sensor that causes two protrusions in the chair's back to vibrate when in the presence of such fields. Others protect against electromagnetic radiation, such as *Loft*, a box atop a ladder that is lined in lead to protect sensitive magnetic recordings, or *Electro-draught Excluder*, a true placebo—an ungrounded, foam-lined "shield" that provides only a false sense of comfort and protection. Responsive objects such as the *GPS Table*, which contains a global positioning sensor that displays its location in the world on an LED display or simply flashes "lost" when it cannot make contact with an orbiting satellite, or *Phone Table*, which is designed to store a mobile phone that causes the table to gently glow when a call is received, elicit behaviors from their users: Do I move the table so it can be "found?" Do I answer the phone or ignore it?

90

Anthony Dunne and Fiona Raby *Diane, Arabella and*
Compass Table 2001 Photo: Jason Evans

92

Anthony Dunne and Fiona Raby *Compass Table* from
Placebo Project 2001 Photo: Jason Evans

Anthony Dunne and Fiona Raby *Emma, Constance
and Electricity Drain* 2001 Photo: Jason Evans

Anthony Dunne and Fiona Raby *Lauren and Electro-*
draught Excluder 2001 Photo: Jason Evans

Anthony Dunne and Fiona Raby *Electro-draught Excluder*
from *Placebo Project* 2001 Photo: Jason Evans

Anthony Dunne and Fiona Raby *Sofie and Loft* 2001
Photo: Jason Evans

Anthony Dunne and Fiona Raby   *Dick and GPS Table*
2001   Photo: Jason Evans

99

100   Anthony Dunne and Fiona Raby   *GPS Table* from
Placebo Project   2001   Photo: Jason Evans

Anthony Dunne and Fiona Raby *Denis, Harry, Lida and Parasite Light* 2001 Photo: Jason Evans

Anthony Dunne and Fiona Raby   *Neil and Nipple Chair*
2001   Photo: Jason Evans

104

Anthony Dunne and Fiona Raby *Nipple Chair* from
Placebo Project 2001 Photo: Jason Evans

Anthony Dunne and Fiona Raby *Tracey and Phone Table*
2001 Photo: Jason Evans

MICHAEL ANASTASSIADES
ANTI-SOCIAL LIGHT, 2001

The *Anti-Social Light* and its antithetic sibling *Social Light* are objects designed to be responsive to a user's behavior. Although a light has an obvious function of illumination, the *Anti-Social Light* performs this task only in the presence of silence. Speech, ambient sound, or noise causes it to dim and eventually switch off. Conversely, the *Social Light* requires sound or conversation to activate it. The solitary act of reading and the conviviality of a dinner conversation suggest two distinct contexts for these lights. This unconventional relationship between people and things intentionally complicates the servile role of products, creating a world in which users cannot simply command an action to occur, but rather one in which their own behavior produces specific effects. The animation of ordinarily inanimate objects introduces an unexpected element of surprise that fundamentally recasts our relationships with products. As Michael Anastassiades explains, "It has very much to do with respect for what the object needs and what it demands, or it won't respond the way you want it to. In an abstract way, it is almost like a companion that behaves a certain way in the house."

Michael Anastassiades *Anti-Social Light* 2001
Photos: Cameron Wittig

MAREK WALCZAK, MICHAEL MCALLISTER, JAKUB SEGEN, AND PETER KENNARD
DIALOG, 2002–2003

Like a regular table, *Dialog* is designed for social interactions, but it utilizes digital technologies and an innovative interface to facilitate learning more about the arts. Gesture recognition and video-tracking software allow multiple users to interact simultaneously with a variety of information appearing on the screen. Using metaphors of water, players can choose artworks by selecting, enlarging, and dragging images from an available "pool" of content to individual "puddles." Connections are made between artworks, creating links among various pieces and users. Additional information can be obtained about the artwork, including related audio and video clips. Another function allows users to print postcards of favorite works. This prototype was commissioned by the Walker Art Center through an international design competition in 2002. *Dialog* counters the isolated and individual interaction – one person, one monitor – that comprises most computer-related scenarios, exchanging the predominant model of personal computing for sociable computing.

Marek Walczak, Michael McAllister, Jakub Segen,
and Peter Kennard *Dialog* 2002–2003

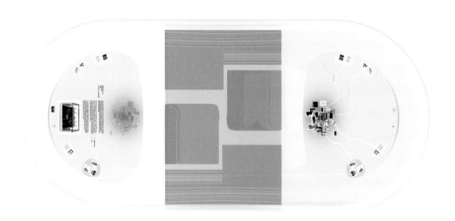

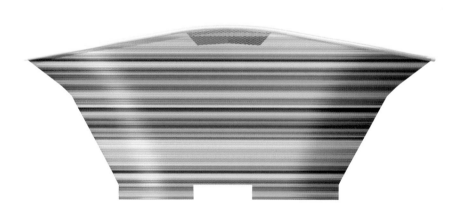

112   Marek Walczak, Michael McAllister, Jakub Segen, and Peter Kennard *Dialog* 2002–2003

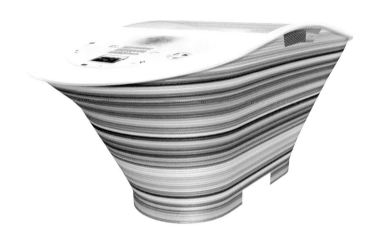

Taking inspiration from inexpensive and improvised shelves – like those made from concrete blocks and wooden boards – *Free Play* is a simple system of parts that can be arranged by the user in configurations that depend on individual storage needs. The system is composed of two elements: miter-cut plastic bands and perforated steel shelves. The bands can be folded or cut in predetermined intervals to form variously sized storage compartments. Magnetic pins embedded in the plastic connect to the metal shelves. Like Blu Dot's other furnishings, *Free Play* encourages consumers to participate in the realization of the final design. It avoids the do-it-yourself limitations of typical "flat pack" furniture, which people assemble per instructions, with a more flexible and open-ended system of choices. The variable nature of this system allows users to make mutable compositions that can be as willful as they choose.

Blu Dot *Free Play* 2003 Photos: Cameron Wittig

Blu Dot *Free Play* 2003 Photo: Cameron Wittig

WWW.FORTUNECOOKIES.DK
FELT 12x12, 2001

While modern industrial manufacturing ensures that each product will be exactly the same, the increasing desire for customization and personalization requires new and different approaches. Envisioned as a "building block," *Felt 12x12* consists of small squares of felt that can be assembled by the user, thus allowing the consumer to determine the type and style of the garment. The drab gray material is in stark contrast to the bright creative potential of the product, as witnessed by results such as a bridal gown and groom's suit, a workman's vest, or an elegant dress. Such an approach rethinks the traditional relationship between designer and user, or as fortunecookies states: "A designer's role in society is to create a framework, within which consumers can define shape and form for themselves. The principle is to give the consumer the freedom to create their own style and thereby define their own lifestyle."

www.fortunecookies.dk *Felt 12x12* 2001
Photos: Gabriella Dahlman

 www.fortunecookies.dk *Felt 12x12* 2001
Photos: Gabriella Dahlman

FRANK TJEPKEMA AND PETER VAN DER JAGT, <u>DO BREAK</u>, 2001
MARIJN VAN DER POLL, <u>DO HIT</u>, 2001
THOMAS BERNSTRAND, <u>DO SWING</u>, 2001

The do create range of products is the brainchild of the Dutch advertising agency KesselsKramer, known for its edgy and conceptual approach to youth-oriented campaigns, and Droog Design, a collective of independent designers that dominated the 1990s design scene with surprising twists on conventional objects. In the words of do create, the central principle is the desire to "make the products come alive." The do philosophy—as in "do-it-yourself"—demands user participation. A cube of thin steel pounded into a chair, a vase that can be broken to form a crackle pattern but does not shatter, and a ceiling light you can swing from— all of these exemplify do's participatory spirit. do create overturns conventional notions of modern industrial manufacturing whereby identical objects are made en masse. do create products are in essence incomplete objects, which can become one-of-a-kind items, personalized and customized through individual acts of consumption.

Frank Tjepkema and Peter van der Jagt *do break* 2001
Photo: Bianca Pilet

127

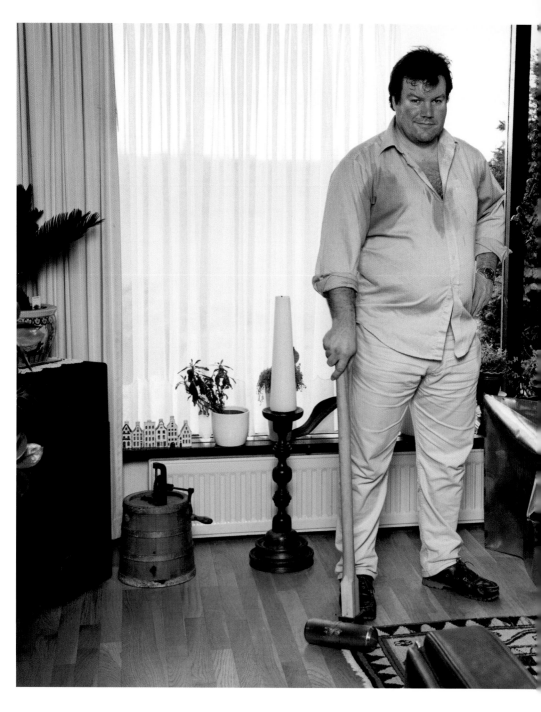

Marijn van der Poll *do hit* 2001 Photo: Bianca Pilet

Thomas Bernstrand *do swing* 2001 Photo: Bianca Pilet

PAOLO ULIAN
GREEDINESS METER, 2002

Paolo Ulian explores the humorous potential of product design with such creations
as *Double Match* (a two-headed match-
stick), *Bath Mat* (a fusion between a pair
of slippers and a bathroom floor mat), and
Greediness Meter. The latter represents
the conflation of different forms: the
seductive lure of chocolate in a shape
that inhibits its intake. Molded in white
and dark chocolate, it dutifully records
its own consumption as it gauges our
insatiable appetite.

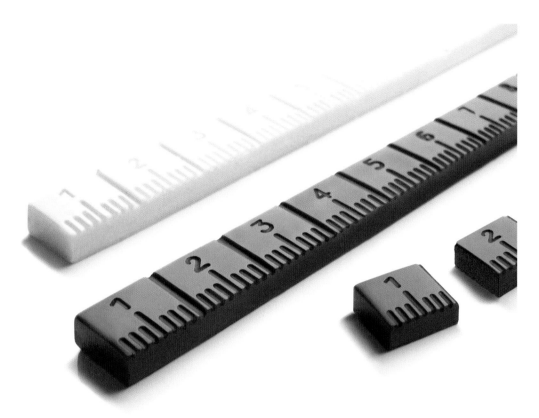

Paolo Ulian *Greediness Meter* 2002

134   Paolo Ulian *Greediness Meter* 2002

ELEPHANT DESIGN
INSIPID COLLECTION, 2000

Tokyo-based elephant design has inverted the conventional notion of supply and demand, and expanded the concept of build-to-order with a design-to-order approach. Their Web site, cuusoo.com, facilitates the production of new consumer goods by establishing a virtual marketplace. Online consumers are presented with a collection of potential or virtual products, or can suggest ones they would like to buy. Development is comprehensive, ranging from finding the right manufacturer to giving form to the desired product to estimating costs and determining the overall feasibility. When enough orders are received, production begins, using Japan's extensive network of small subcontracted manufacturers. Among its product ideas is the *Insipid Collection* of consumer goods that includes, for example, a vacuum cleaner, a rice cooker, a phone, and a fax machine. As the title of the collection suggests, the sleek, white, minimal forms are devoid of the eye-catching but superfluous details typically found on other consumer goods. Distilled to their essence, *Insipid* products are a counterpoint to the pop sensibility of much contemporary Japanese design, whether cartoon anime figures or the ubiquitous Hello Kitty.

elephant design *Microwave* from *Insipid Collection*
2000

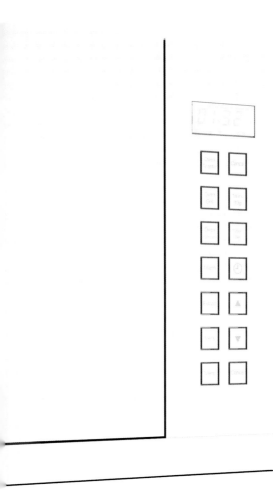

elephant design *Rice Cooker* from *Insipid Collection*
2000

elephant design *Cordless Phone* from *Insipid Collection*
2000

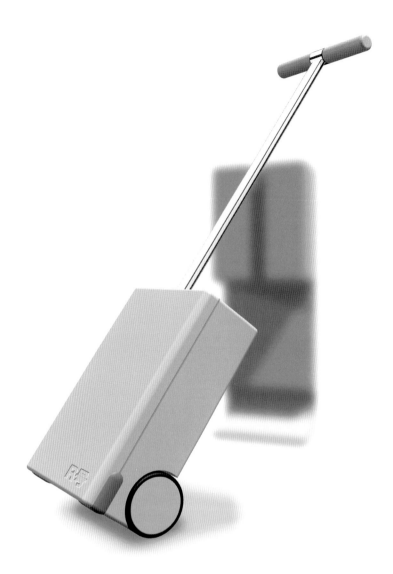

142   elephant design   *Vacuum Cleaner* from *Insipid Collection*
2000

elephant design *Phone* from *Insipid Collection* 2000

elephant design *Paper Circulator* from *Insipid Collection*
2002

PORTABLE STRUCTURES

R&SIE...

HABITAT FURTIF, 1998

Originally created for the exhibition *Propos Mobile*, *Habitat Furtif* (no longer extant) traveled the streets of Paris propelled by bicycle power. Inside, a narrow space accommodates one person with fixtures for sleeping and washing. A plastic panel roof captures borrowed daylight or streetlight. On the outside, its surface is covered by mirrored plastic, reflecting and distorting the environments it passes. As it moves through the city, its solidity dissolves, creating in its wake a rippling and disorienting view of once familiar spaces. In this way, it acts in an almost anti-spectacular fashion, both revealing and concealing aspects of the world around it. It is difficult not to draw parallels between the stealth-like quality that effectively disguises this portable dwelling and the condition of homelessness itself, at once visible and often ignored or rendered invisible.

146

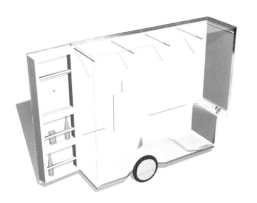 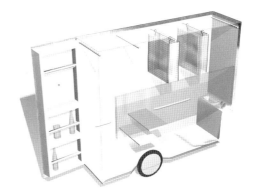

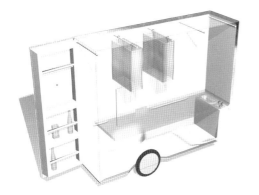 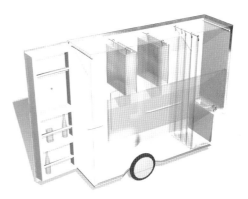

R&Sie... *Habitat Furtif* 1998

R&Sie... *Habitat Furtif* 1998

MARKKU HEDMAN

KESÄ-KONTTI (SUMMER CONTAINER), 2001

The traditional Finnish vacation cabin has been reinterpreted as a transportable house for two. Markku Hedman's *Kesä-Kontti*, or *Summer Container*, operates like a matchbox—when unoccupied it forms a closed wooden cube that can be transported on a trailer. Upon reaching its intended location, the container can be "unpacked": the living compartment can be pushed out and the shutters and doors opened. Intended for fishing trips, camping, or holiday relaxation, it contains a kitchen, work table, convertible living/sleeping area, and storage space. Cooking and sanitary functions can be added and electricity is provided by solar panels or wind turbine.

Markku Hedman *Kesä-Kontti* (*Summer Container*) 2001

Markku Hedman *Kesä-Kontti* (*Summer Container*) 2001

Markku Hedman   *Kesä-Kontti* (*Summer Container*)   2001

LOT-EK

MOBILE DWELLING UNIT (MDU), 2003

International trade among many different countries around the world necessitated the development of universal, integrated methods of transporting goods. Taking such systems and standards as its starting point, LOT-EK has converted an existing shipping container into a personal living space, or *Mobile Dwelling Unit* (*MDU*). Envisioned for use with today's increasingly nomadic lifestyles, the *MDU* can be easily transported via truck, ship, and train. When it reaches its destination, it is housed in a "harbor," a multiple-level steel rack capable of holding many such units. Once securely in place, all systems (water, sewer, power, data) can be connected. When in use, cuts in the metal walls of the container allow sub-volumes to be pushed out to greatly expand the available space. Inside, each sub-volume contains a functional element for living, whether a storage space, kitchen, or media center. Designers Giuseppe Lignano and Ada Tolla imagine the state of change not only within the *MDU* itself but also among the many units in the harbor: "Like pixels in a digital image, temporary patterns are generated by the presence and absence of *MDU*s in different locations along the rack, reflecting the ever-changing composition of these colonies scattered around the globe."

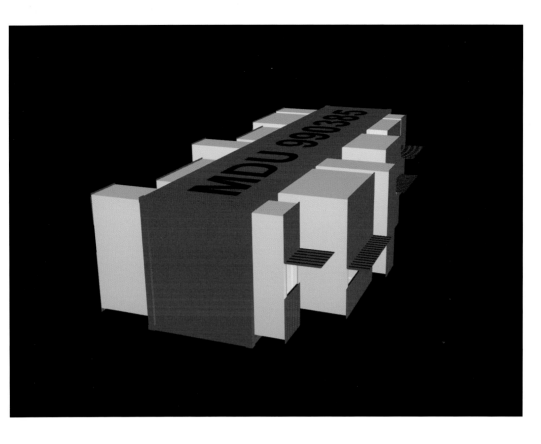

LOT-EK *Mobile Dwelling Unit* 2003 Organized by
the University Art Museum, University of California,
Santa Barbara, and LOT-EK, New York

159

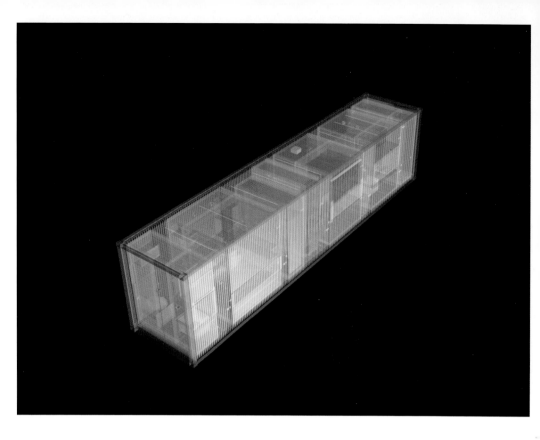

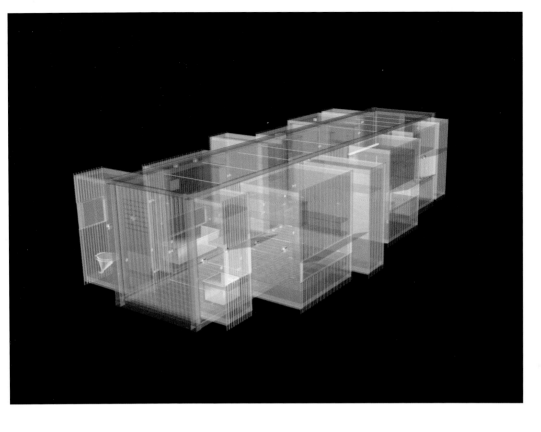

161

    LOT-EK *Mobile Dwelling Unit* 2003

LOT-EK *Mobile Dwelling Unit* 2003

MARKKU HEDMAN

ETANA (SNAIL), 2003

Etana (*Snail*) is a concept for a new type of dwelling that is modular, portable, and transformable. Consisting of three elements – a shell, a skin, and infill – *Snail* is highly flexible and can be used as a home or office in urban or rural locations. As Markku Hedman says, "*Snail* is your office. It is for living. It is a cloth that you wear for protection. It is a capsule you take everywhere." The shell is available in fixed lengths that can be easily trans- ported by trucks, ships, and trains. Once situated, an inflatable and insulated skin is unfurled that greatly expands the living area. The infill system consists of furniture and various fixtures such as appliances, storage cabinets, showers, and toilets. Numerous fixture configurations are possi- ble, allowing for extensive customization of the space; the furniture is designed to be easily movable, accommodating daily changes to the interior.

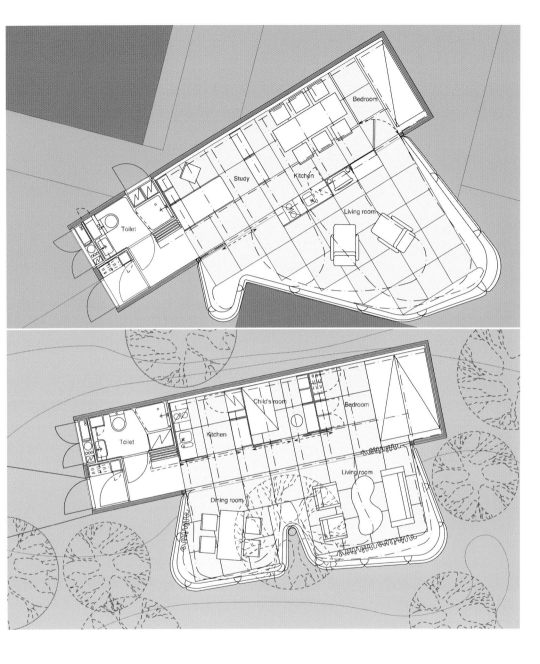

Markku Hedman *Etana* (*Snail*) 2003

Markku Hedman *Etana* (*Snail*) 2003

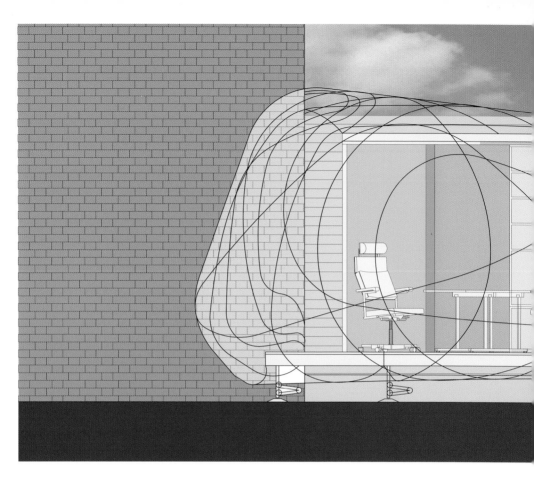

Markku Hedman *Etana* (*Snail*) 2003

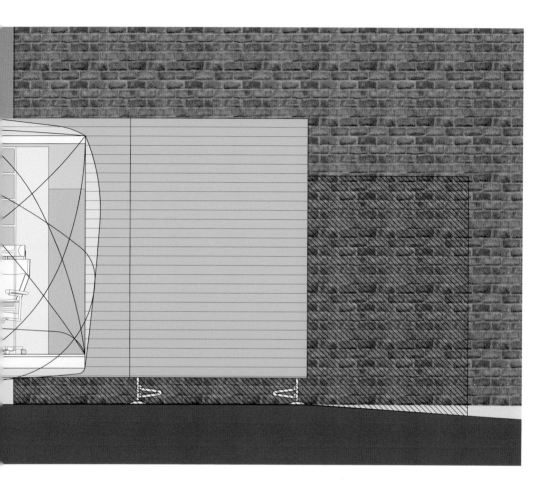

171

JENNIFER SIEGAL, OFFICE OF MOBILE DESIGN
PORTABLE HOUSE, 2001

Our conventional image of a mobile home is often limited to either stereotyped notions of a trailer park or the mundane efficiency of portable classrooms. While *Portable House* is in fact a variant of these forms, its design and premise is much more contemporary and engaging. With its use of ecosensitive materials, minimalist interior styling, and affordable pricing, it is designed to appeal to those seeking more mobility and flexibility in their lives. The forty-foot-long and twelve-foot-wide *Portable House* can accommodate both living and working scenarios. The units can be individually situated or grouped together to create common areas such as courtyards or gardens. The structure can be readapted, reoriented, and relocated to a variety of environments, from open landscape to an urban setting. This peripatetic vision of freedom and movement with opportunities for communal togetherness underscores the nomadic traditions of early civilization – an image Jennifer Siegal sees in the figure of the *Portable House*, "the way it moves across and rests lightly upon the landscape, providing a provocative counterpoint to the status-quo housing model."

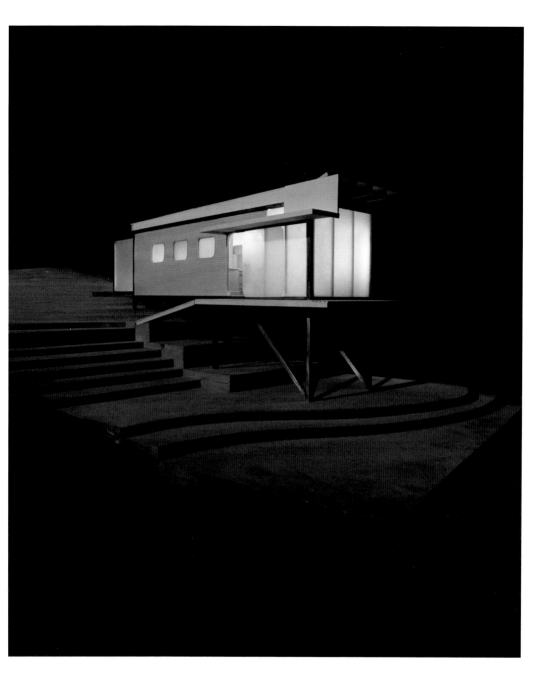

Jennifer Siegal *Portable House* 2001

Jennifer Siegal *Portable House* 2001

Jennifer Siegal   *Portable House*   2001

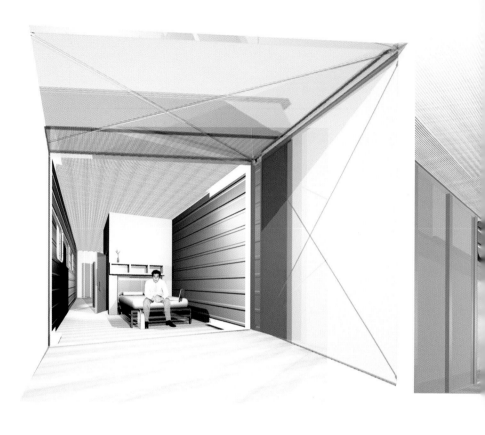

Jennifer Siegal *Portable House* 2001

ALEJANDRO STÖBERL

PREFABRICATED WOODEN HOUSE, 2001

Argentinian architect Alejandro Stöberl has experimented with several structures that provide modern living accommodations at more affordable prices. *Prefabricated Wooden House* is constructed entirely of premanufactured components and is transported via truck to the desired location. Conceived of as an alternative to the cabin or beach home, it can be installed by four people in four days, making it a much faster and less labor-intensive activity than traditional house construction. Approximately six hundred fifty square feet in size, the dwelling contains two occluded sections, one the kitchen and the other a bath. Otherwise, the entire volume is glass-walled from floor to ceiling, allowing for seamless visual access between occupant and nature. A series of retractable, folding wooden shutters along the front and back of the house provides protection and privacy when drawn.

Alejandro Stöberl *Prefabricated Wooden House* 2001

Alejandro Stöberl *Prefabricated Wooden House* 2001

SHIGERU UCHIDA
GYO-AN PAPER TEA HOUSE, 1995

The ancient Japanese tradition of the tea ceremony is a meditation on social interactions, a way of honoring guests. *Gyo-an*, one of three designs by Shigeru Uchida for contemporary tea houses, is composed of wooden strips that intersect in a tangled web of triangles forming starlike patterns. Heightening the feeling of lightness are the perforated, latticed walls, which circumscribe a boundary in flux between inside and outside, public and private, and visual dynamism and sensory contemplation. Noting that "a tea room is not a fixed aesthetic world," Uchida uses conventional materials such as cedar, bamboo, stone, and rice paper in extraordinary ways, creating a structure that responds to the increasingly impermanent nature of contemporary life. Thus, each room is easy to assemble, dismantle, and move, offering a particularly modern approach to this most ancient of rituals.

Shigeru Uchida *Gyo-an Paper Tea House* 1995
Photo: Nacása and Partners, Inc.

185

186

Shigeru Uchida   *Gyo-an* (1995) (center), one of three
Paper Tea Houses   Photo: Nacása and Partners, Inc.

ALLAN WEXLER

GARDENING SUKKAH, 2000

Sukkot is an autumnal harvest festival commemorating the temporary shelters used by the Jews during their forty-year exodus in the wilderness. A sukkah is a temporary outdoor structure erected for the festival where meals can be served. An important element is the roof, which is typically formed as a lattice framework providing shade without obscuring the night sky. Allan Wexler's *Gardening* *Sukkah* provides not only the structure for the festival's observance (including a retractable roof to allow sunlight and moonlight) but also the implements necessary to cultivate the crops as well as the furnishings needed for dining. Wexler's design is a deft blend of forms – at once recalling the typical the garden shed and possessing the same mobility as the wheelbarrow.

Allan Wexler *Gardening Sukkah* 2000

190   Allan Wexler *Gardening Sukkah* 2000

192   Allan Wexler *Gardening Sukkah* 2000

SHIGERU BAN
PAPER LOGHOUSE, 1995

In 1995 the Hyogo-Ken Nanbu earthquake struck Japan, inflicting considerable damage to the city of Kobe. Responding to this humanitarian crisis, architect Shigeru Ban devised the *Paper Loghouse* as a temporary shelter for the homeless. The use of paper tubes for the walls and sandbag-filled plastic Kirin beer crates for the foundation enables the structure to be assembled by unskilled volunteers. The fabric roof, windows, and doors allow the house to be used for longer periods of time in a variety of climatic conditions, and its materials can be easily recycled, allowing for a more ecologically sound and timely dispersal process. Like his designs of more permanent buildings and spaces, Ban's *Paper Loghouse* evokes traditional Japanese architecture but with a distinctly modern sensibility, transforming humble materials into strong structural statements.

Shigeru Ban *Paper Loghouse* 1995
Photo: ©Takanobu Sakuma

195

196

Shigeru Ban *Paper Loghouse* 1995
Photo: ©Hiroyuki Hirai

MARTÍN RUIZ DE AZÚA
BASIC HOUSE, 2000

Weighing but a few ounces, *Basic House* is the most portable of homes, able to be carried in a pocket like a handkerchief. Fabricated from a reversible lightweight metallic polyester, each side possesses a different thermal property: silver protects against the heat and gold insulates against the cold. A slight breeze will inflate the house, and body and solar warmth keep it aloft during the day. In the evening as temperatures fall, the cube deflates around the inhabitant, forming an insulating covering. The same material has been used in other scenarios, such as an emergency blanket for a stranded motorist, a warm covering for the homeless, or a protective mantle for outdoor concertgoers. Yet Martín Ruiz de Azúa's approach expands the material's conceptual and aesthetic potential. With the portability of a garment and the functionality of a tent, *Basic House* is intended as a statement about personal mobility and individual freedom. "I love freedom and nature. The idea of ambling off wherever I please without having to make sure in advance I have somewhere to take shelter is a really thrilling one," he says.

Martin Ruiz de Azúa *Basic House* 2000
Photo: Daniel Riera

200   Martín Ruiz de Azúa *Basic House* 2000
                                            Photos: Daniel Riera

202

Martín Ruiz de Azúa *Basic House* 2000
Photo: Daniel Riera

MULTIFUNCTIONAL OBJECTS

203

MORENO FERRARI, C.P. COMPANY
TENT, KITE, AND SLEEPING BAG
FROM TRANSFORMABLES COLLECTION, 2001

A cloak becomes a kite, a rain suit doubles as a tent, and a jacket becomes a sleeping bag. This shape-shifting alchemy is performed in Moreno Ferrari's collection of transformable garments for Italian sportswear enterprise C.P. Company. Adapting to a variety of conditions at the will of the wearer, this apparel uses the language of fashion to tell a much more poetic story of human needs and desires. Objects in the collection embrace the increasingly nomadic and solitary conditions of contemporary urban life. The dual nature of these garments points to the tension inherent in the modernist doctrine that the form of an object be expressive of its function. What form does an object take when it expresses multiple functions? Ferrari answers this question through ingenious designs that reconcile these conflicting expectations, with each state being harmoniously resolved.

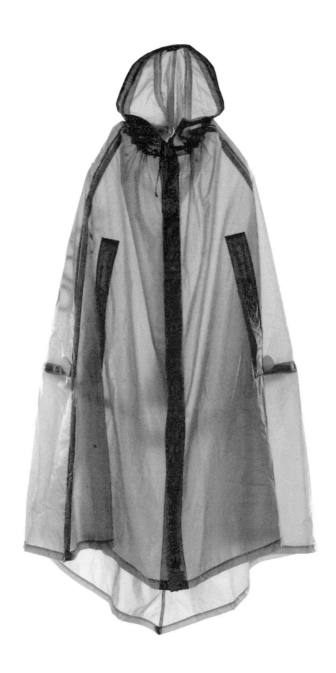

Moreno Ferrari *Kite* from *Transformables Collection* 2000

Moreno Ferrari *Kite* from *Transformables Collection* 2000

Moreno Ferrari *Kite* from *Transformables Collection* 2000

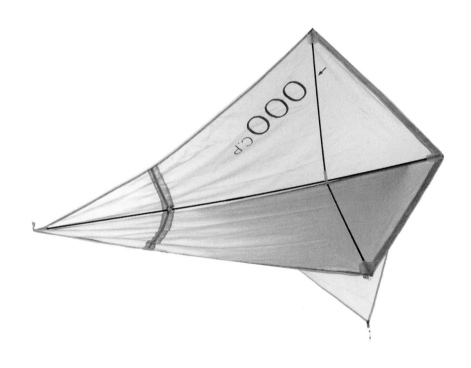

Moreno Ferrari *Tent* from *Transformables Collection* 2000

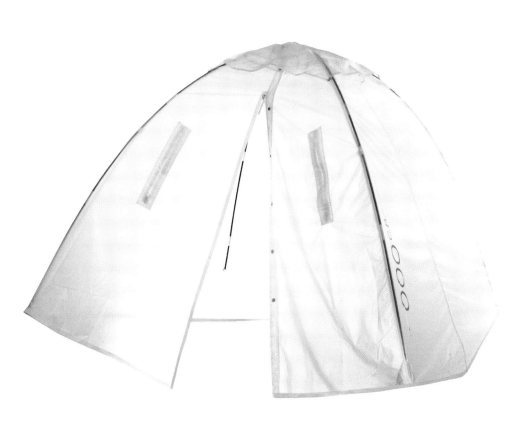

Moreno Ferrari *Sleeping Bag* from *Transformables Collection* 2000

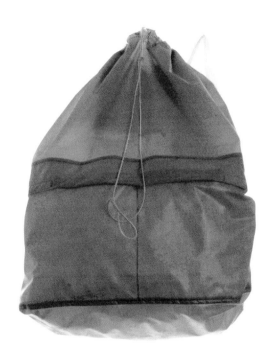

JULIAN LION BOXENBAUM

<u>**RUGELAH CHAIR,**</u> **2000**

Faced with limited space as a design student living in New York, Julian Boxenbaum created the *Rugelah Chair* as an exercise in multifunctionality. It can be configured by the user in various ways to create different seating options as well as unrolled completely to make a long sleeping surface. The chair's iconic form evokes the rolled pastry of the same name. While the chair expresses the portability and space efficiency of a carpet, it was actually inspired by Boxenbaum's experience as a nature guide: "There is a rule in wilderness trekking: One object has to serve at least two functions, or you don't take it. In design, that's considered a compromise of both form and function, but I don't buy it."

Julian Lion Boxenbaum *Rugelah Chair* 2000
Photo: Cameron Wittig

215

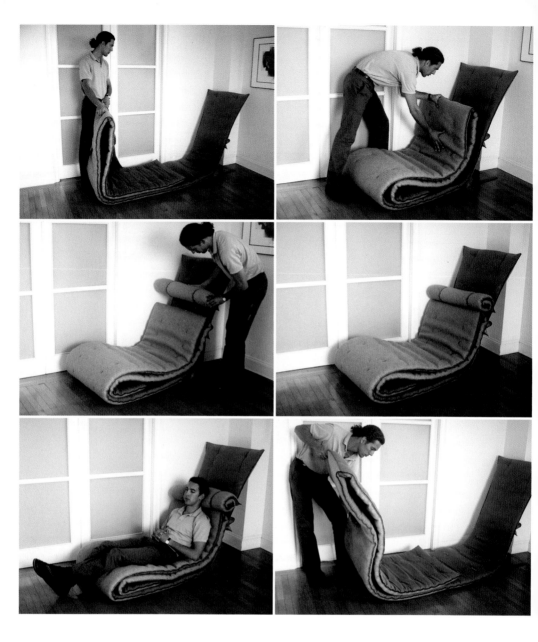

216
Julian Lion Boxenbaum *Rugelah Chair* 2000

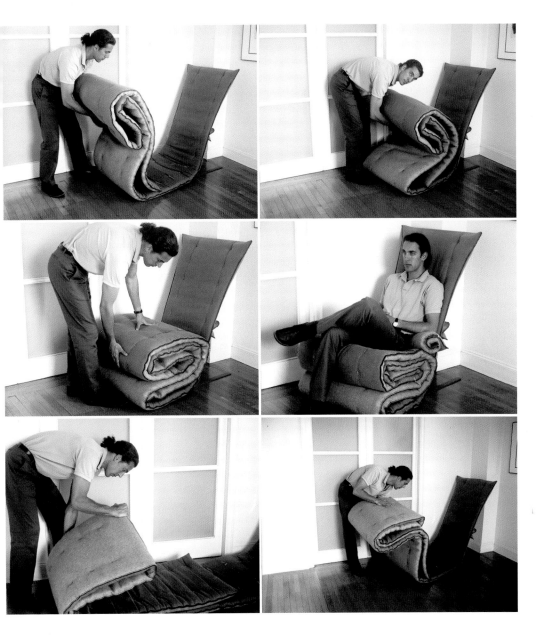

218   Julian Lion Boxenbaum *Rugelah Chair* 2000

PAOLO ULIAN
CABRIOLET/OCCASIONAL TABLE, 2000/2002

Paolo Ulian's *Cabriolet/Occasional Table* was chosen as the best piece at the 2000 Milan Furniture Fair's Salon Satellite, the furniture industry's most celebrated event. *Cabriolet* integrates three discrete furniture typologies – the bench, the storage unit, and the table – in one multifunctional design. Its typical appearance as a simple occasional table can be transformed when its grooved wooden top is pulled back to reveal a shallow storage unit beneath, or when the top is lifted so a metal support positioned to form a seat back turns it into bench. Like other multifunctional furnishings, its flexible design provides a more spontaneous or improvisational solution to the typical problems of tight living situations, whether the need for additional seating for guests or a convenient place to hide tabletop items when they arrive.

Paolo Ulian *Cabriolet/Occasional Table* 2000/2002

KOERS, ZEINSTRA, VAN GELDEREN
TUMBLE HOUSE, 1998

Originally commissioned as an alternative to traditional storage sheds, Koers, Zeinstra, van Gelderen's *Tumble House* responds to its context – the changing character of the garden. Not only are the natural elements (trees, shrubs, flowers) in constant flux, but so too are things such as benches, tables, chairs, and umbrellas, which are often rearranged at will. Taking inspiration from the idea that "a garden house should not be an extension of the fixed house but more or less a piece of garden furniture," the designers created a six-sided polyhedron. It can be tumbled onto any of its sides, and each orientation creates a unique interior configuration with an entrance, or door, that in other positions functions as a window, skylight, closet, table, or bed. The house's geometry was shaped by giving each side obtuse angles, thereby minimizing corners and facilitating the tumbling action.

Koers, Zeinstra, van Gelderen *Tumble House* 1998

223

224   Koers, Zeinstra, van Gelderen *Tumble House* 1998

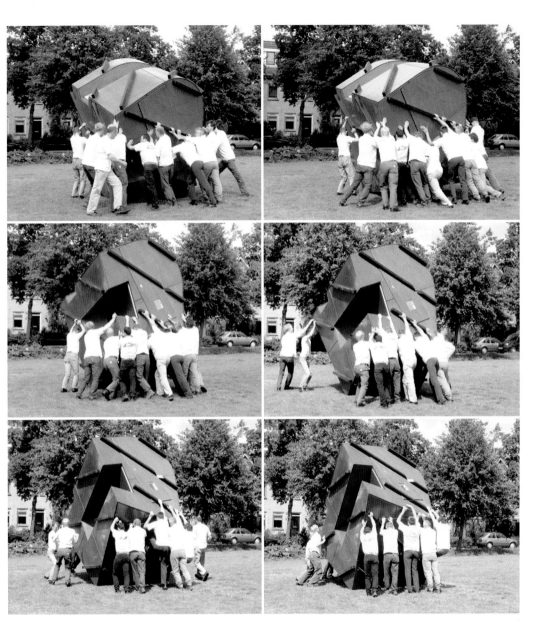

226   Koers, Zeinstra, van Gelderen *Tumble House* 1998

SU11 ARCHITECTURE+DESIGN
COMPOSITE HOUSING, 2002

Composite Housing updates prefabrication and mass-customization ideas for the residential housing market. With its most recent version, *CHP2*, su11 creates components that can be combined in multiple ways to effectively fashion one continuous habitable environment. These elements challenge the autonomy of rooms, instead suggesting a continuum of "in-between spaces" stretching through or becoming part of a single, expansive component. This new spatial configuration emphasizes the continuity of shape, the fluidity of space, and the articulation of differences. su11 makes surface and texture integral in the overall concept, acknowledging the emotional connection people have with materials (identifying them as cozy, relaxing, luxurious, upbeat, and so on). Because it is possible for materials to possess varying properties within the same surface (such as soft and hard, smooth and rough, opaque and translucent), materiality and tactility become important strategies that signal, for instance, programmatic changes. Beginning the design process with the bath, for example, it is possible to generate the rest of the design from elements that comprise it: tile can be integrated into the adjoining areas, blurring the distinctions between them. *CHP2* offers a highly customizable range of possibilities and affords opportunities to explore new housing types in an individual way.

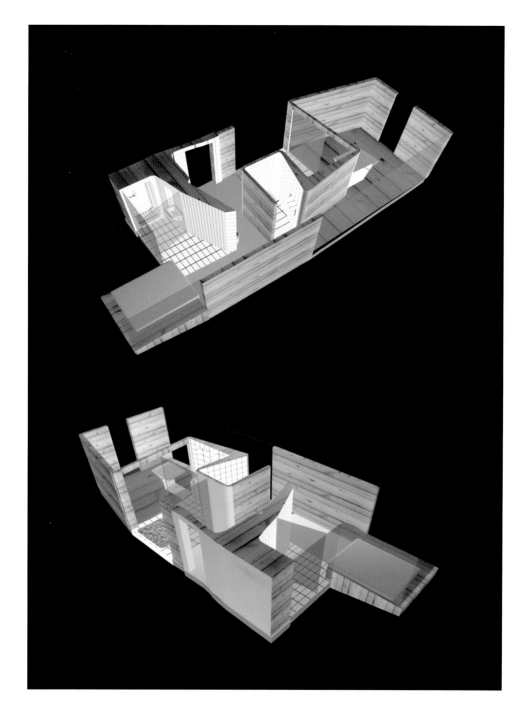

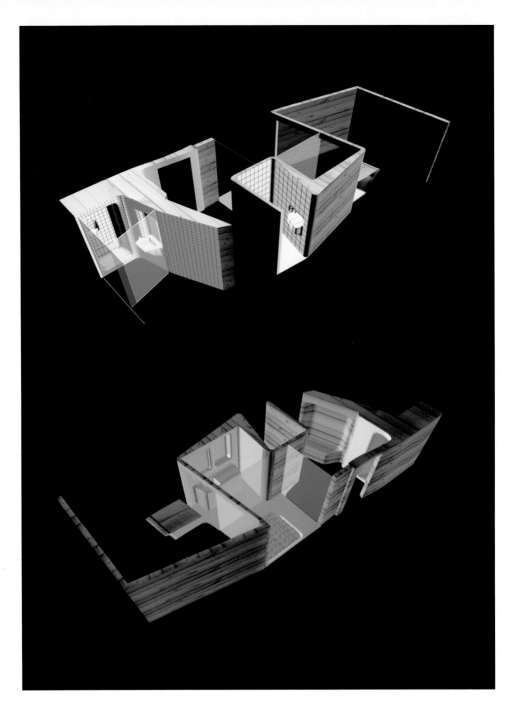

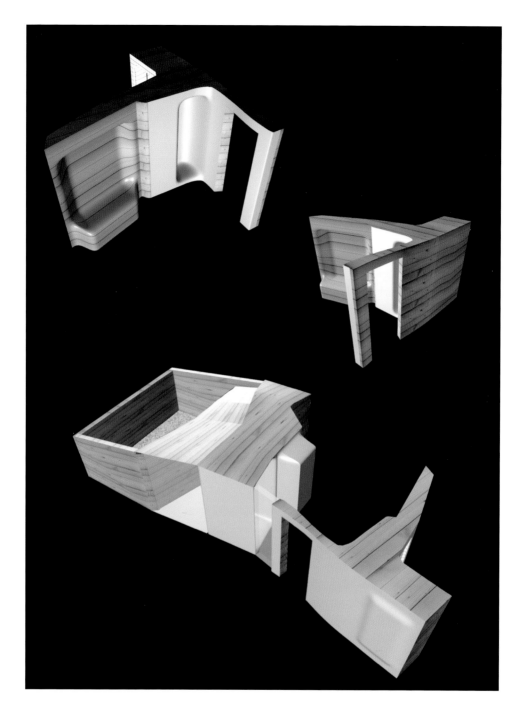

231

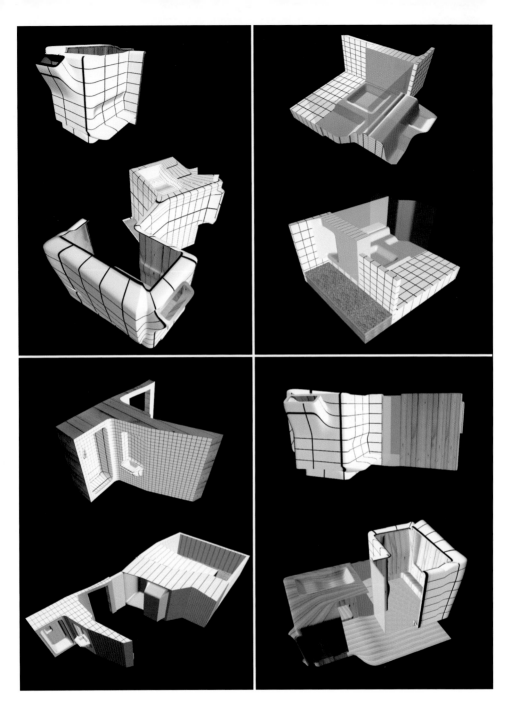

232   su11 architecture+design *Composite Housing* 2002

TRANSFORMING THE EVERYDAY

ATELIER BOW-WOW

<u>**MOTH HOUSE**</u>, 2000

Situated in the town of Karuizawa, Japan, *Moth House* is Momoyo Kaijima and Yoshiharu Tsukamoto's aptly named architectural renovation of a traditional structure built in 1962. Atelier Bow-Wow is known for its innovative design of typically small Japanese houses. *Moth House* refers to one its first occupants, a lepidopterist, who attracted various specimens by spotlighting sections of a white wall at night.

Taking their cues from this wall and the particular history of the home, the architects enveloped the south side of the house in a translucent polycarbonite shell. The resulting "cocoon" protects and preserves the original structure while allowing the outside in through the interplay of dappled light and the fluttering shadows of branches against the surface of the house.

234

Atelier Bow-Wow *Moth House* 2000
Photo: ©Takashi Homma

Atelier Bow-Wow *Moth House* 2000
Photo: ©Takashi Homma

Atelier Bow-Wow *Moth House* 2000
Photo: ©Takashi Homma

JURGEN BEY

KOKON CHAIR, 1997–1999

Under the auspices of Droog Design, the Dutch collective that created a sensation in the world of design in the 1990s, Jurgen Bey produced the *Kokon* series of furniture pieces. Employing a technique used to "mothball" or store military equipment and aircraft, he sprayed a synthetic elastic fiber coating onto existing pieces of wooden furniture. The resulting forms capture the ghostly presence of what lies beneath, creating a distinctive appearance for otherwise commonplace objects. Since the coating fills gaps and spaces between elements, hybrid but continuous forms can be achieved, such as the fusion of a chair and table. Consistent with Droog's quintessentially "dry" sense of humor and straightforward, uncomplicated approach to design, Bey's *Kokon* collection eschews stylistic mannerisms in favor of a more conceptual and direct vocabulary.

Jurgen Bey Furniture from the *Kokon* series 1997–1999

DOUG GAROFALO
MARKOW RESIDENCE, 2001

Long considered the site of relentless uniformity, the American suburbs have not been a hotbed of architectural innovation. In spite of this reputation, Garofalo Architects has been redesigning several suburban houses in the greater Chicago area—transforming once-staid structures into dynamic spatial compositions. Rather than creating a whole new house or enveloping the entire building with a fresh body, the design for *Markow Residence* adapts to key elements of the original home and takes its cues from its surrounding context. While the 1960s-style twin gables are retained, the new roof's double "V" profile offers a formal counterpoint. Eschewing the traditional front-to-back orientation pattern of the neighborhood, the house contorts itself to open the inside to outside views and light sources. Within, the major living spaces are freed from their conventional partitioning to create free-flowing spaces in place of enclosed rooms. The radical geometry of the *Markow Residence*, realized through the aid of the computer, is itself a commentary on the true nature of the contemporary suburb – no longer rigidly homogenous, but a complex interplay of diverse elements.

242

Doug Garofalo *Markow Residence* 2001
Photo: ©William Kildow Photography

Doug Garofalo *Markow Residence* 2001
Photo: ©William Kildow Photography

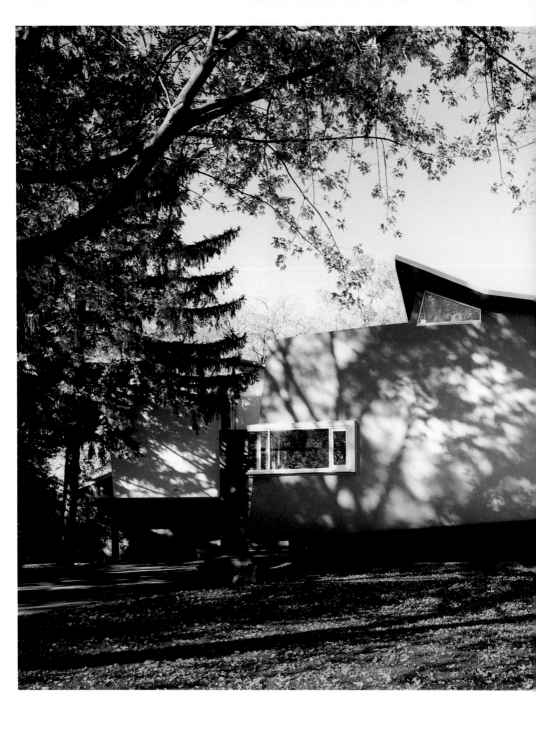

Doug Garofalo *Markow Residence* 2001
Photo: ©William Kildow Photography

Doug Garofalo *Markow Residence* 2001
Photo: ©William Kildow Photography

RACHEL WHITEREAD
DAYBED, 1999

The London-based furnishings company SCP commissioned artist Rachel Whiteread to design a daybed. Renowned for her castings of commonplace objects and spaces, Whiteread created a design that draws upon her previous sculptures of beds. Unlike most sculptures, Whiteread's works are often casts of the negative or empty area in and around objects. Thus the four round holes in *Daybed* are understood as the space once occupied by bedposts, while the surface's bands can be seen as an impression of the underside of a bed. *Daybed* plays on this fluctuating notion of absence and presence and spatial ambiguity, occupying the space where an actual, other bed would have been.

Rachel Whiteread *Daybed* 1999

NUCLEO
TERRA: THE GRASS ARM-CHAIR, 2000

The designers at Nucleo proclaim: "*Terra* is not a finished product, it is an idea." Indeed, the user is the catalyst by which the concept becomes reality. Supplied with a kit that includes a cardboard frame and a box of grass seeds, the customer is instructed to grow his/her own chair. As a seamless part of the landscape, *Terra* ingeniously blends the artificial and the natural. Over time the cardboard frame disintegrates, leaving behind a structure of earth and grass. In order to retain its functionality, the chair requires maintenance, such as watering and trimming. The level of user involvement in the chair's realization expresses the designers' intention to make us aware of how objects come into being. Nucleo asks: "Which is the best way to learn about an object? To feel it? Surely to construct it. There is no greater form of intimacy for an object than to be created."

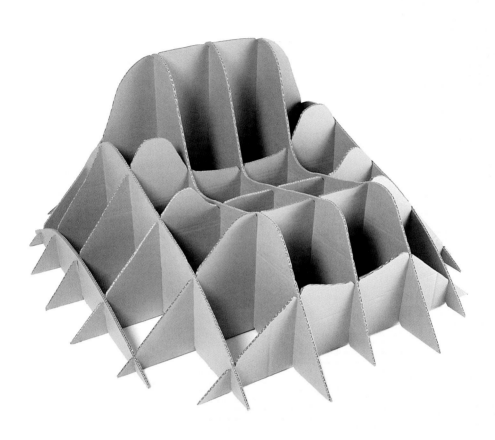

Nucleo *Terra: The Grass Arm-chair* 2000
Photo: Maria Elena Moretti

254   Nucleo   *Terra: The Grass Arm-chair*   2000
Photo: Maria Elena Moretti

MARCEL WANDERS

AIRBORNE SNOTTY VASES, 2001

Sinusitis, Pollinosis, Coryza, Influenza, and Ozaena – the polysyllabic names of nasal ailments double as the titles of designer Marcel Wanders' series of vases produced by Cappellini. Based on the mucus expelled by a sufferer of one of the aforementioned conditions, the Snotty Vases utilize the latest in imaging and fabrication technology. A scan is taken when a subject sneezes, a single particulate is selected, and the image greatly enlarged. This picture is transferred to a computer, where it is modeled into a three-dimensional form. Next, it is transformed into an actual object using a process called selective laser sintering, which melts a powdered plastic layer by layer into the final shape. Wanders fuses the natural and the artificial in the most direct way, using technology to give form to the invisible. The resulting objects are strange yet graceful instantiations of otherwise commonplace afflictions.

Marcel Wanders *Sinusitis* from *Airborne Snotty Vases*
2001 Photo: Maarten van Houten

Marcel Wanders *Pollinosis* from *Airborne Snotty Vases*
2001 Photo: Maarten van Houten

Marcel Wanders   *Coryza* from *Airborne Snotty Vases*
2001   Photo: Maarten van Houten

259

Marcel Wanders *Influenza* from *Airborne Snotty Vases*
2001 Photo: Maarten van Houten

Marcel Wanders *Ozaena* from *Airborne Snotty Vases*
2001 Photo: Maarten van Houten

CONSTANTIN BOYM AND LAURENE LEON BOYM
BUILDINGS OF DISASTER, 1998–2002

In 1998 Constantin and Laurene Leon Boym began work on *Buildings of Disaster*, a series of scale miniatures of infamous sites – souvenirs to mark the end of the millennium. Commemorating various political, social, and ecological disasters, the collection includes the Unabomber's cabin, Chernobyl, the Oklahoma City Federal Building, and the Alma Tunnel, site of Princess Diana's death. As product designers and architects, the Boyms were attracted to the idea that calamities transform ordinary places and anonymous structures into icons and historical markers of our time. The series speaks to what they term the "American-ness" of catastrophe as dealt with by popular culture, particularly its portrayal in the media. "Disaster and tragedy are already part of the popular culture, so this project actually comments on that reality – not just on the disaster itself, but on the response to the disaster," says Constantin Boym. They struggled with the particular problem of what, if anything, should be done after the terrorist attacks on the World Trade Center and the Pentagon in 2001. The World Trade Center had already been included in the series because of the 1993 bombing. Should two of the most recent and significant tragedies in America's history be ignored? After much consideration and soul-searching, including requests from former occupants of the twin towers, they decided to produce both commemorative pieces, with the proceeds going to charity.

Constantin Boym and Laurene Leon Boym *Buildings of
Disaster* (*Triangle Shirtwaist Company, March 25, 1911*)
1998–2001 Photo: Cameron Wittig

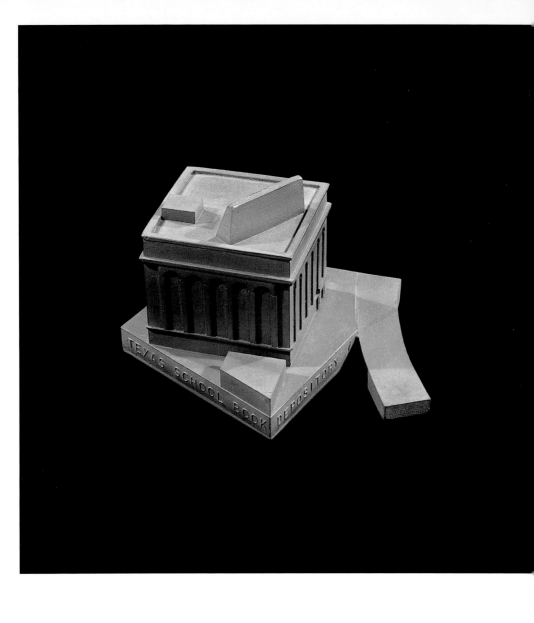

264

Constantin Boym and Laurene Leon Boym *Buildings of
Disaster (Texas School Book Depository, November 22,
1963)* 1998–2001 Photo: Cameron Wittig

Constantin Boym and Laurene Leon Boym *Buildings of*
Disaster (*The Watergate, June 17, 1972*) 1998–2001
Photo: Cameron Wittig

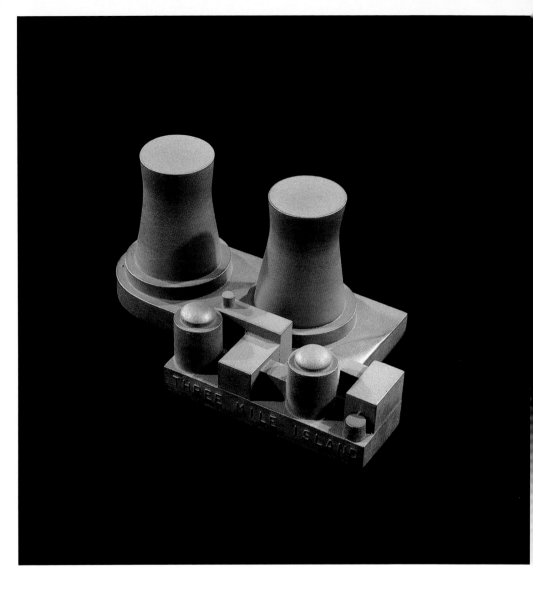

266

Constantin Boym and Laurene Leon Boym *Buildings of
Disaster* (*Three Mile Island, March 28, 1979*) 1998–2001
Photo: Cameron Wittig

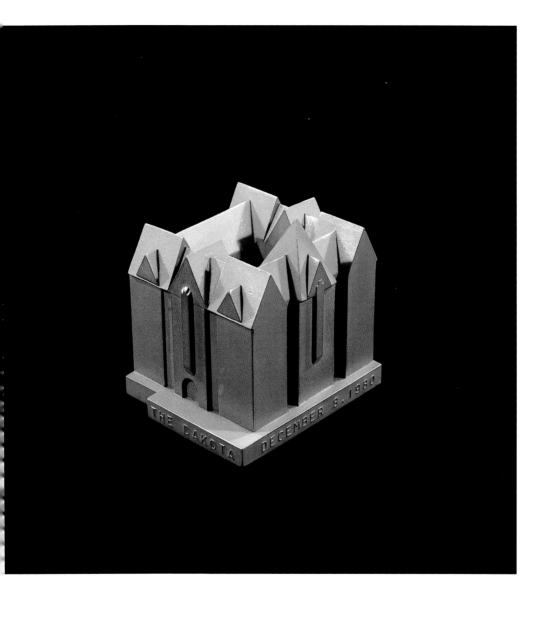

Constantin Boym and Laurene Leon Boym *Buildings of*
Disaster (*The Dakota Building, December 8, 1980*)
2002 Photo: Cameron Wittig

267

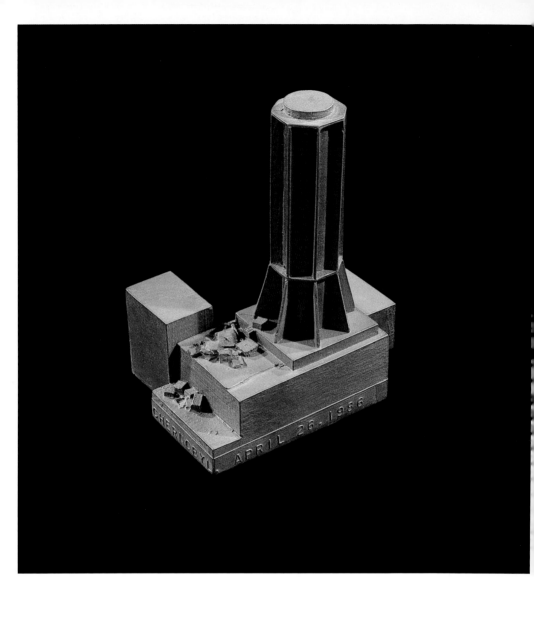

268

Constantin Boym and Laurene Leon Boym *Buildings of Disaster* (*Chernobyl, April 26, 1986*) 1998–2001
Photo: Cameron Wittig

Constantin Boym and Laurene Leon Boym *Buildings of Disaster (The World Trade Center, February 26, 1993)* 1998–2001 Photo: Cameron Wittig

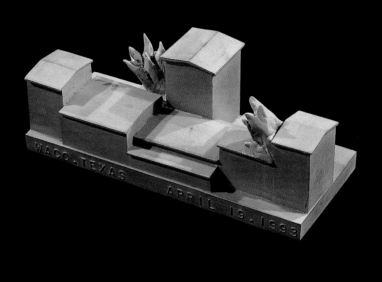

Constantin Boym and Laurene Leon Boym *Buildings of
Disaster* (*Waco, Texas, April 19, 1993*) 1998–2001
Photo: Cameron Wittig

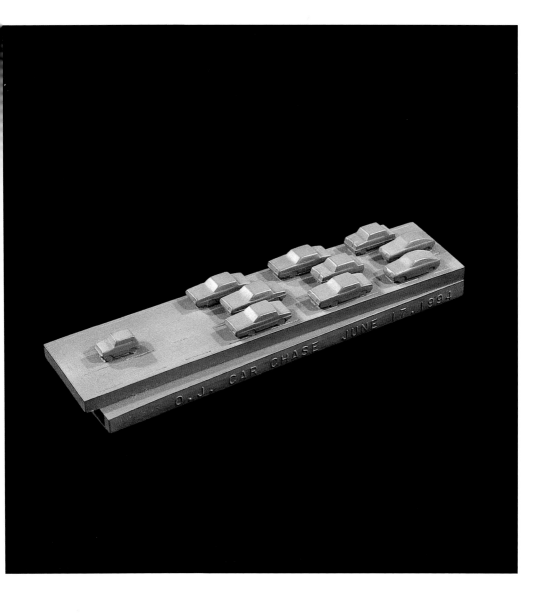

Constantin Boym and Laurene Leon Boym *Buildings of*
Disaster (*O.J. Car Chase, Los Angeles, June 17, 1994*)
1998–2001 Photo: Cameron Wittig

271

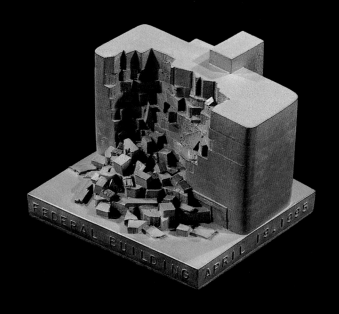

272

Constantin Boym and Laurene Leon Boym *Buildings of
Disaster* (*Oklahoma City Federal Building, April 19,
1995*) 1998–2001 Photo: Cameron Wittig

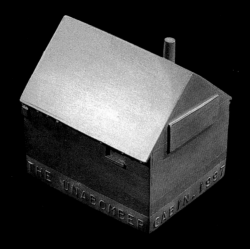

Constantin Boym and Laurene Leon Boym *Buildings of
Disaster* (*The Unabomber's Cabin, 1997*) 1998–2001
Photo: Cameron Wittig

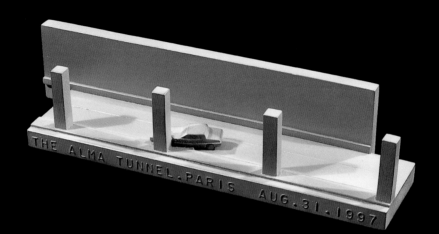

274

Constantin Boym and Laurene Leon Boym *Buildings of Disaster* (*The Alma Tunnel, Paris, August 31, 1997*) 2002
Photo: Cameron Wittig

Constantin Boym and Laurene Leon Boym *Buildings of
Disaster* (*Texas A & M Bonfire, November 18, 1999*)
1998–2001 Photo: Cameron Wittig

275

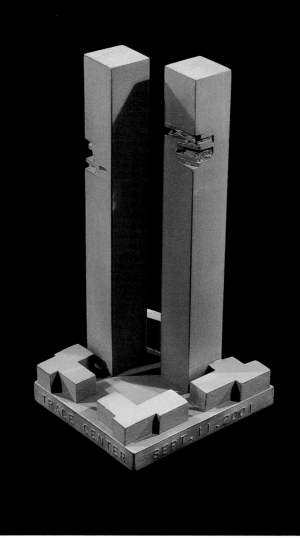

276

Constantin Boym and Laurene Leon Boym *Buildings of Disaster* (*The World Trade Center, September 11, 2001*) 1998–2001 Photo: Cameron Wittig

Constantin Boym and Laurene Leon Boym *Buildings of
Disaster* (*The Pentagon, September 11, 2001*)
1998–2001 Photo: Cameron Wittig

CONSTANTIN BOYM

<u>UPSTATE</u>, 2002

Inspired during trips to the family's country home in upstate New York, Constantin Boym created *Upstate*, a series of commemorative ceramic plates. Through photographic images of various small towns and rural landscapes, the series bestows on otherwise anonymous places the significance implied by the traditional collectable plate of famous tourist sites.

As a keepsake of travel experiences, the souvenir serves as evidence that one was there. The views depicted in *Upstate* are distinctly roadside vistas that, in the words of the designer, reflect an "understated and very American beauty . . . [but] there was always something slightly off-key, either a jumble of telephone wires overhead, or a 'wrong' car on the road."

Constantin Boym *Upstate* (*Mohonk, NY*) 2002
Photo: Cameron Wittig

280

Constantin Boym *Upstate* (*High Falls, NY*) 2002
Photo: Cameron Wittig

Constantin Boym   *Upstate* (*Ellenville, NY*)   2002
Photo: Cameron Wittig

281

Constantin Boym   *Upstate* (*Kerhonkson, NY*)   2002
Photo: Cameron Wittig

Constantin Boym *Upstate* (*Kippelbush, NY*) 2002
Photo: Cameron Wittig

283

284

Constantin Boym   *Upstate* (*Pataukunk, NY*)   2002
Photo: Cameron Wittig

JOP VAN BENNEKOM
<u>RE-</u>, 1997–2002

RE–, a magazine about everyday life, began in 1997 as a final project for Jop van Bennekom, then a student at the Jan van Eyck Akademie, a graduate program in the Netherlands. Acting as writer, editor, publisher, designer, and photographer for the magazine, he integrated the typically separate functions of publishing in a quest to link these diverse activities and draw together his own interests. Inverting the conventional idea of a magazine's subjects and readership, he presents not a world of celebrities and prepackaged media events, but rather stories about and conversations with friends and ordinary people. Thematic in nature, *RE–* covers topics such as the home ("Living Apart Together"), mass media ("Inbetween"), sex ("On Sex"), and even boredom ("Boring!"). In the words of its designer, *RE–* is "a platform for daily experience, not a vehicle for the extreme, the new, or the stereotypical, but for the marginal, the ordinary, and the common."

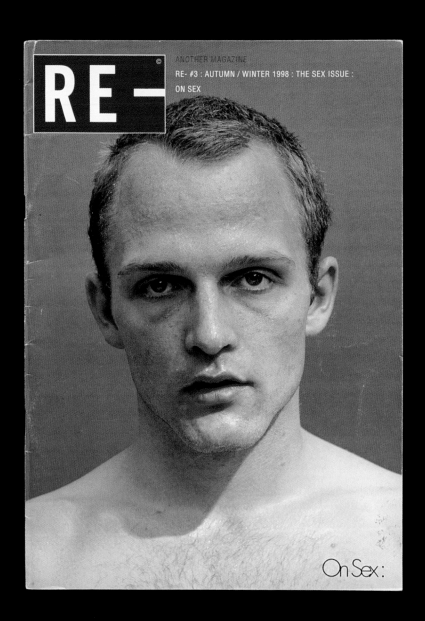

On Sex:

Jop van Bennekom *RE‑* Magazine #3: The Sex Issue
"On Sex" August 1998 Photos: Cameron Wittig

RE-

© ANOTHER MAGAZINE

RE- #3 : AUTUMN / WINTER 1998 : THE SEX ISSUE :

ON SEX

On Sex :

Jop van Bennekom   *RE–* Magazine #6: The Manic Issue
"The Information Trashcan"   March 2001
Photo: Cameron Wittig

Jop van Bennekom *RE– Magazine #4: Boring!* May 2000

Photo: Cameron Wittig

Talkin'around...
Reflection.

Page 12 out of 84

Jop van Bennekom   Spread from *RE–* Magazine #4:
Boring!   May 2000   Photo: Cameron Wittig

alkin'around...
art 3: Room Seven, the attendant reflects.
y Hans Aarsman.

This very ~~interesting~~, impotant etc.

uestion: which are in the majority: solariums or mopeds?
nswer: solariums.
/ouldn't it be better instead of demanding an answer to inquire after a way of finding an answer?
stead of asking: Does a hair grow out of the root or from the tip?
sk: How could we determine if a hair grew out of the root or from the tip?

must be all of two years ago since I got rid of y car. It was a Golf Diesel, twelve years old but ll in good repair. I bought it new, always check- the oil, drove neither too fast nor too slow, 5,000 kilometers on the clock, petrol consump- on of 21 kilometers to the liter, no rust. I sold it r a thousand guilders, would have fetched a bet- r price if I'd put an ad in the paper, between fif- en hundred and two thousand guilders for sure.

ccording to statistics, a car covers an average of ghteen thousand km per year. Eighteen thousand r year, that's 1500 km per month. Within the ty limits not as fast as on the open road, let's ssume the average speed is 65 km per hour. 65 n per hour, therefore it takes 23 hours to cover 500 kilometers. The average motorist spends 23 ours per month behind the wheel of his car. ltogether running a car costs about 750 guilders r month, and we're not talking about a big lercedes. Check the Consumer Guide if you on't believe me. The Golf cost me 550 guilders r month and a car in the mid-price range like a issan Primera, a Renault Laguna or an Opel ectra costs you 750 guilders. Petrol, insurance, epreciation, road tax, parking license, mainte- ance, the familiar items. To earn that amount an verage employee has to work 50 hours, which e'll add to the 23 he's already spent behind the heel of his car, amounting to a total of 73 hours. On top of that we have the traffic jams, trips to and from the garage, washing the car, giving granny a lift or helping friends without a car to move house, the times you would have gone for a walk in the neighborhood if you hadn't got a car, but now you drive to the beach, and the search for a parking space – quarter of an hour in the center of town is nothing. Altogether 15 hours, and that's a modest estimate. A total of 88 hours per month is spent on the car, and all that just to cover those 1500 kilometers. Divide those 1500 kilometers by 88 hours and you arrive at an actual speed slightly exceeding 17 kilometers per hour.

Phew, let me take the weight off my feet. Except in museums. I never heard anyone say: phew, let me take the weight off my feet. But otherwise, everywhere you go, the whole day: phew, let me take the weight off my feet. Foreigners are differ- ent. They sit down, but they don't say anything. Every Dutchman says it at least three times a day – is that a fair estimate? Worldwide therefore it will be heard – how many of us are there, 15 mil- lion – 45 million times per day. There are 86,400 seconds in a day. A fact I've experienced first hand, 86,400 seconds tick away before the day is through. If I'm quiet, and my pulse rate drops to 60 beats per minute, then my heart beats exactly the same number of times per day: 86,400. 1440 is a number helpful to have at hand, so that you don't first have to multiply 24 hours by 60 min- utes – and that times 60 heartbeats, is 86,400. How many times during the time it takes for my heart to beat once, does someone somewhere in Holland say: phew, let me take the weight off my feet? 45 million divided by 86,400...Is 520. Actually it's not too bad, it's all in the mind. The mind starts sputtering when things go well, it can't take it if everything goes too smoothly. Does your mind really know how to cope with prosperity? Prosperity and good fortune. When things threaten to go well, the mind tends to drift off. As if it needs something to sink its teeth into. It might be a food shortage, even a state terror campaign, or because it's time to arm yourself but not just to drift aimlessly. It can't cope. Better to face a major war. Up until now, whenever I've thumped somebody, it served to clear the air afterwards. A small dose of violence can really help to clear up personal conflicts. All the more when guns speak. A gigantic tangle of nuances, interpretations, rationalizations and relativity is split between pro and contra. Us or them. Free rein for instinct. But the peace has barely been signed before instinct crawls back into its hole. And later when it's allowed out again under supervision, it will have to wait just like everyone else for the traffic lights to change from red to green. The streets full of attaché cases and prams. Behave yourself and do your best, early to bed, watch your language.

'age 13 out of 84

On the magazine cover:

Format.

RE–

Re-Magazine #7
Difficult Magazine
Autumn 2001
Re-View
HfL 17,50 / 8 Euro

07

—RE-VIEW—

Jop van Bennekom *RE–* Magazine #7: Re-View
September 2001 Photo: Cameron Wittig

Re-Magazine #23
Spring 2007

Re-Magazine
Established 1997

NL/ B/D -€ 8,00
F - € 9,50
UK - £5,95

IT'S SPRING
TWO THOUSAND SEVEN

(2007)

No. 5 Mother.

Page 28 out of 84

Jop van Bennekom   Spread from *RE–* Magazine #5: The
Anti-attitude Issue "Re-connect yourself!"   November 2000
Photo: Cameron Wittig

Jeweight

Re-connect attempt No. 5:
Mother.
Re-connect with your mother.
Explain yourself, show her your work.
Meet your mother.

Text: Lernert Engelberts/ Gijsbert van der Wal.
Fotografie: Marnix Goossens/ Misha de Ridder.

MVRDV
DUTCH PAVILION, EXPO 2000, 2000

Created to represent the Netherlands at *Expo 2000* in Hanover, Germany, the *Dutch Pavilion* is a microcosm of the country's landscape, containing elements of air, water, flowers, and forest. Arranged in a vertical stack measuring one hundred thirty feet high, each of the pavilion's six layers offers a distinct environment, whether the windmill farm atop the roof, the water-washed walls of a cinema, a forest, or the lower level's artificial "dunes." Conceived as a microecology, the pavilion underscores the *Expo*'s environmental theme. Wind turbines on the roof move cool air over a basin of rainwater that trav-els down the sides of the glass facade to the floor below. This water is used to irrigate the forest and is passed through a biomass filter before it is returned to the roof, where the cycle is repeated. MVRDV's design echoes the Dutch mastery in transforming — literally re-creating — nature, whether reclaiming land from the sea or propagating new species of tulips. In a country as dense as the Netherlands, the architects contend that extra space can be found through expanding space vertically. However, they rightfully ask: "Can increasing population density coexist with an increase in the quality of life?"

MVRDV *Dutch Pavilion, Expo 2000* 2000

MVRDV *Dutch Pavilion, Expo 2000* 2000
Videographer: Hans Werleman

MVRDV

PIG CITY, 2001

The Netherlands is the one of Europe's major pork producers. In 1999, there were 15.2 million pigs and 15.5 million people living in the country, an astounding ratio that reflects the increasing demands placed on natural resources. Recent public concern about animal diseases and the use of antibiotics as well as the desire for an all-grain diet complicate an already complex problem. The video *Pig City* was produced by MVRDV in order to explore the fundamental question: "Is it possible to compact all pig production within concentrated farms, therefore avoiding unnecessary transportation and distribution, and hereby reducing the spread of diseases?" In order to preserve land for other uses, the resulting scheme creates vertical farms that integrate the total production of pork, containing systems for growing food, a self-sufficient method to recycle fertilizer, and a communal slaughterhouse. As with many of its projects, MVRDV examines the generative possibilities of statistical information – how data can determine the parameters for design.

300

MVRDV *Pig City* 2001
Animation: Wieland and Gouwens, Rotterdam

302

MVRDV *Pig City* 2001
Animation: Wieland and Gouwens, Rotterdam

R&SIE...

SCRAMBLED FLAT, 2001

Situated in the Swiss village of Evolène, known for its prized Herens cows, *Scrambled Flat* is an exploration of contemporary farm dwellings that blends human and animal habitation. The proposal contains space for three small apartments, a barn for a dozen cows, a hayloft, wood storage, and an apiary. From the outside, *Scrambled Flat* takes its unique form from the bales of hay found throughout the region. Inside, its seemingly odd mix of functions references traditional methods of agricultural life, where the basement serves as a barn and the body heat of the animals warms the areas above. This compact, multifunctional space is both primitive and futuristic, drawing upon ancient traditions and digital modeling programs. It is a particularly local approach to techno-farming, with R&Sie... responding not to the problems of the global economy's vast corporate farms but rather to the small-scale, centuries-old farm and its vernacular traditions.

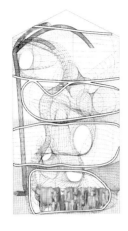
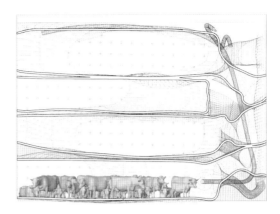
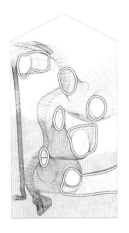
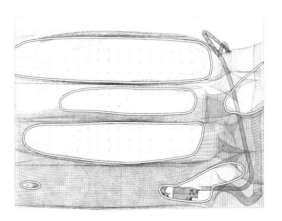

R&Sie... *Scrambled Flat* 2001

R&Sie... *Scrambled Flat* 2001

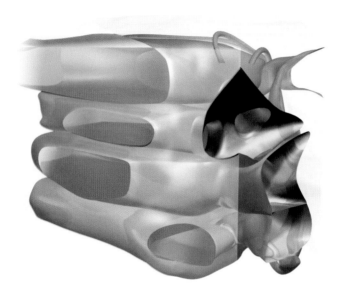

R&Sie... *Scrambled Flat* 2001

MICHAEL ANASTASSIADES
Born 1968, Athens, Greece
Originally trained in civil engineering, Michael Anastassiades received his master's degree in industrial design from the Royal College of Art in London. He established his studio in 1994, and has since shown his work internationally in both group and solo exhibitions, including *Lost and Found* (British Council, 1999) and *Stealing Beauty: British Design Now* (Institute of Contemporary Arts, London, 1999). The projects created by this London-based designer have brought clever innovation to the customary object. Merging sleek designs with new technologies, Anastassiades transforms cups, tables, and lights into items of unconventional engagement and wonder. For example, *Alarm Clock Table* (1998) is a simple bedside table that vibrates at a preset time. Its function requires the interaction of another object; for instance, a set of keys that rattles, thereby producing the

sound that will awaken the user. Building on this dislocation of a common object's function, he designed a prototype for a message cup (1994), which holds words instead of water. With the aid of a thin electronic card embedded in its base, one can "fill" the cup with a message that can then be "poured" out by another. With this twist, the cup's meaning is no longer dependent on convention, but rather on those who use it. Working collaboratively with Dunne & Raby, also featured in *Strangely Familiar*, Anastassiades helped create *Weeds, Aliens, and Other Stories* (1998–2000). The trio designed objects that mediate our relationship with nature, such as *Talking Tabs*, plant labels that recite recipes or poems, and *Rustling Branch*, a motorized branch that rustles every forty seconds, an aural alternative to the traditional vase of flowers. A commitment to the idea that design can change our behavior and attitudes informs Anastassiades' ongoing investigations of the psychological relationships we establish with everyday objects.

ATELIER BOW-WOW

Founded 1992; based in Tokyo, Japan

Momoyo Kaijima

Born 1969, Tokyo, Japan

Yoshiharu Tsukamoto

Born 1965, Kanagawa, Japan

An interest in ways that contemporary urban conditions help shape the built environment led Momoyo Kaijima and Yoshiharu Tsukamoto to form Atelier Bow-Wow in 1992. Based in Tokyo, the studio has developed a growing international reputation for its innovative designs as well as for its investigations into what they term *da-me* (no-good) architecture. In their book *Made in Tokyo* (2001), Tsukamoto and Kaijima, with Junzo Kuroda, document *da-me* structures most architects would ignore, including such oddities as a shopping center crowned by a roller coaster and a graveyard situated over a tunnel. Another project, *Pet Architecture Guidebook* (2001), celebrates some of Tokyo's smallest structures: a repair shop on a sidewalk so narrow that motorcycles cannot be housed in it, or small diners that are essentially countertops adjacent to open kitchens. The lessons their studies offer are not those of conventional aesthetics, but rather those that demonstrate highly economical and efficient solutions to problems of limited space and resources. Championing layered, mixed-use structures, Atelier Bow-Wow is among Japan's new generation of acclaimed designers. *Mini House*, which was awarded Tokyo Architect's Gold Medal prize in 1999, is a project that implements some of Atelier Bow-Wow's primary concerns, including the maximum economy of space. Similarly, a proposal the firm has submitted for an outdoor bath takes advantage of an under-utilized space atop an incinerator smoke-stack. The studio's work has been featured in exhibitions in Tokyo, Munich, Rotterdam, Paris, London, and most recently in Minneapolis in the Walker Art Center's *How Latitudes Become Forms: Art in a Global Age* (2003).

SHIGERU BAN

Born 1957, Tokyo, Japan

Shigeru Ban studied architecture at the Southern California Institute of Architecture (SCI-Arc) in Los Angeles and the Irwin S. Chanin School of Architecture at Cooper Union in New York, where he received his degree in 1984. Ban returned to Japan and opened his private practice in 1985, embarking on an experimental trajectory that would become the hallmark of his work. Investigating new uses of existing technology and materials, he dared to employ paper as a primary building material. He first worked with paper tubes, using them as frames for temporary shelters in Rwanda while he served as a consultant for the United Nations High Commissioner for Refugees. When an earthquake devastated Kobe in 1995, Ban participated in relief efforts in Japan and also established the nongovernmental organization Voluntary Architects' Network (VAN). Through the coordinated efforts of the congregation, volunteers, and financial donors, he created *Paper Church* (1995), an evocative structure comprised of paper-tube columns, an outer skin of corrugated polycarbonite sheeting, and a tented roof, as well as his *Paper Loghouses* (1995). Ban's design for the *Japanese Pavilion* for *Expo 2000* in Hanover, Germany, reflects his environmental concerns and innovative approach to architecture. In order to eliminate the vast amount of waste of both materials and energy usually generated by the production of temporary pavilions, his design considers the building's entire life cycle. Working with renowned German architect and structural engineer Frei Otto, Ban designed a seventy-meter-long, vaulted space made entirely of specially treated paper tubes. The material not only alleviated great expense and energy in the building's construction, but upon demolition, the structure's parts were either recycled or returned for reuse. Ban's highly refined and innovative houses include the iconic *Curtain Wall House*, with its retractable fabric facade, *Wall-Less House* (1997), which employs sliding panels rather than walls or mullions, and his series of *Furniture Houses* (1995–1996), which utilizes prefabricated units that function as both structural and space-defining elements. His work has been exhibited and published internationally and among his major awards are the Japan Institute of Architecture's 3rd Kansai Architect Grand Prize (1996), the Best Young Architect Prize (1997), and the 18th Tohoku Architecture Prize (1998). Most recently, Ban has collaborated with THINK, a group of architects and engineers led by Rafael Vinoly and Frederic Schwartz, on the redesign of New York's World Trade Center site. Their proposal was one of two finalist designs.

JOP VAN BENNEKOM

Born 1970, Scherpenzeel, the Netherlands

Since receiving his postgraduate laureate from the Jan van Eyck Academie in Maastricht, the Netherlands, Jop van Bennekom has been involved in the development of several magazines. He generated the first issues of *RE–* magazine during his graduate school studies. Rejecting stereotypical, commercial images and media-driven stories, *RE–* is a quarterly publication about daily life, for and about ordinary people. Van Bennekom served for a time as art director of *Blvd.*, a popular Dutch magazine, but soon returned to more alternative forms of editorial work. After relaunching *RE–*, he and Eric Wong redesigned *Forum*, a Dutch architecture magazine. Interdisciplinary in scope and based on the design principles of "reshape" and "rethink," the publication follows van Bennekom's approach to magazine production, which involves a greater integration of design and editorial work. Wong and van Bennekom were awarded the prestigious Rotterdam Design Prize in 2001 for *Forum*'s synthesis of form and content. His continuing interest in divergent ideas and alternative representations and audiences led him to begin yet another publishing venture: he and Gert Jonkers established the quarterly *Butt* for gay men in 2001. They maintain total control over its publication, from inception to distribution, and have stripped it bare of the genre's mainstream pinups and glossy advertisements. Whether placing the focus back on everyday life or unvarnished sexuality, van Bennekom's publications evoke the personal.

JURGEN BEY

Born 1965, Soest, the Netherlands

Rotterdam-based Jurgen Bey views his design process as one that "transforms questions into objects." The items he creates amaze, disconcert, and provoke, and his interest in their life stories and varying contexts of use brings a narrative element to his work. Bey's strategy of reinvesting everyday objects with new lives can be seen in a number of works. With *Broken Family* (1999), for instance, he has turned old porcelain services into updated versions of themselves with new silver-plating. In 1999, along with Martí Guixé, Hella Jongerius, and Marcel Wanders, he participated in a commission to revitalize the Oranienbaum, a seventeenth-century castle and estate in Germany. As part of this effort, his *Tree Trunk Bench* (1999) wittily re-creates the common park bench by attaching antique chair backs cast in bronze to a fallen tree. As part of the same project, he created *Gardening Bench* (1999), using the natural waste of the garden—hay, clippings, fallen leaves—which when compressed and extruded forms a bench that will eventually decompose, suggesting an endless cycle of production and reclamation. Bey's inventive designs have been exhibited internationally, and he continues to share his enthusiasm and ideas with students at the Design Academy in Eindhoven, the Netherlands, where he was a student in the early 1990s. Among his other realized works are the interior design of the Wedding Room in Utrecht's City Hall, the seating for the Rietveld Pavilion of Centraal Museum, Utrecht, and a shop-window concept for Levi's and Droog Design.

BLU DOT

Founded 1996; based in Minneapolis, Minnesota

Maurice Blanks
Born 1964, Midland, Texas
John Christakos
Born 1964, Oneida, New York
Charles Lazor
Born 1964, Bernardsville, New Jersey

Approaching design from the inside out, the three principals of Blu Dot, sculptor John Christakos and architects Charles Lazor and Maurice Blanks, share a decidedly populist bent. Blue Dot initially began as an idea the three Williams College undergraduates entertained for a number of years, and has since materialized into an award-winning design firm of international acclaim. By integrating design and manufacturing and placing production, packaging, and shipping at the fore of their concerns, they have been able to consistently meet their founding goal: to produce affordable modern design. Sharing an admiration for a few notable mid-century modernists, including Alvar Aalto and Charles and Ray Eames, Blu Dot has embraced the values of good design by producing quality pieces at affordable prices. Adopting the flat-pack approach for ease of distribution and reduced transport costs, the firm consciously engages the consumer in the realization of the finished piece. This is particularly true in such works as *2D/3D* (2000), a series of desk accessories purchased as flat, perforated-metal pieces that must be folded into shape, and in *Free Play* (2003), a flexible storage system whereby the customer chooses the final configurations. Receiving numerous awards since its founding, from the Best Collection Award by the Accent on Design Show (1998) to the Best of Category: Packaging by *ID Magazine* (2000), Blue Dot has also been an international commercial success. Its pieces are sold throughout the United States, Europe, and Japan, bringing modern design to a wide-ranging public. The firm's work, from furniture to installation design, has appeared in an array of different exhibitions, including, in New York, the Museum of Modern Art's *Workspheres* (2001) and the Cooper-Hewitt National Design Museum's *Skin* (2002), and in Minneapolis, the Walker Art Center's presentation of *The Un-Private House* (2000), and has made its way into the collection of the Musée des Arts Decoratifs de Montréal.

JULIAN LION BOXENBAUM
Born 1972, New York City

Since graduating with a master's degree in industrial design from New York's Pratt Institute in 2000, Julian Lion Boxenbaum has been living and working in Italy. Prior to his graduation, however, he had already won acclaim for his work. His design for *Rugelah Chair* earned him a place in *I.D. Magazine*'s "Top 40 Designers under Thirty" (January/February 2000). This multiuse chair exemplifies Boxenbaum's design interests – which foreground functionality and versatility – that largely developed during his experience as a wilderness guide in upper New England and Canada. Another of his outback-inspired designs, *Crooked Knife*, won an award in the third annual Seki Cut Design Competition (1999). Using a centuries-old Cree

instrument as a point of departure, Boxenbaum adapts the knife as a unique addition to a modern collection of tools. Having begun his career making jewelry, he continues to alter his professional trajectory, reinventing his practice just as he reinvents the utilitarian object. He is planning to launch a transcontinental studio (New York/Milan) with his father, architect Charles Boxenbaum, which will offer a range of services from architecture to interiors and design.

BOYM PARTNERS INCORPORATED
Founded 1986; based in New York City
Constantin Boym
Born 1955, Moscow, Russia
Laurene Leon Boym
Born 1964, New York City

After graduating from the Moscow Architectural Institute, Constantin Boym earned his master's degree in design from Domus Academy in Milan. In 1986 he founded his own practice in New York and since 1995 has been in partnership with Laurene Leon Boym. Exploring a range of items from clocks to kitchen utensils to tourist souvenirs, the Boyms' designs include housewares for Alessi, DMD/Droog Design, and Authentics, as well as watches for Swatch and exhibition and installation designs for Vitra and the Cooper-Hewitt National Design Museum. Since its founding, the Boym studio has promoted a "culture-driven" approach to its work, seeking to reveal the intrinsic beauty of the quotidian object. This approach can be seen in works such as *Tin Man* (1994), a canister that resembles a soup can but is made from stainless steel; *Benza* (1999), a series of vases made from standard PVC pipes; or a set of polypropylene containers for the company Authentics that recalls the collectable refrigerator glassware of the 1930s. The work of Boym Partners is part of the collections of the Museum of Modern Art, New York; the San Francisco Museum of Modern Art; the Whitney Museum of American Art, New York; the Cooper-Hewitt National Design Museum, New York; and the Musée des Arts Decoratifs de Montréal.

DO CREATE

Founded 2000; based in Amsterdam, the Netherlands

Thomas Bernstrand
Born 1965, Stockholm, Sweden
Peter van der Jagt
Born 1971, Doetinchem, the Netherlands
Marijn van der Poll
Born 1973, Eindhoven, the Netherlands
Frank Tjepkema
Born 1970, Geneva, Switzerland

Dutch advertising agency KesselsKramer created the "do" brand as an "antidote to the one-way world that we live in." It changed the conventional way that brands are developed by starting with a philosophy and then creating products and services in conjunction with various designers. Its philosophy is an open-ended, ever-changing brand that relies on the active participation ("doing") of consumers and others. Recalling the imagination and possibility of childhood, do designers dream of rekindling a personal and exuberant relationship between people and the environments they develop. do create is a collection of products, rather than people, that requires consumer interaction to make those items "come alive." Its first collection, developed

in cooperation with Droog Design, debuted at the 2000 International Furniture Fair in Milan. Fifteen products were presented to critical and popular acclaim. Among the offerings were *do add* (Jurgen Bey), a chair made with one short leg requiring the addition of books or other materials for proper balance, and *do eat* (Martí Guixé), a large sheet of plastic with assorted shapes embossed into the surface allowing the user to cut out plates, saucers, and trays. Following its debut, the do create collection traveled to other international venues, including the Kunsthal Rotterdam, Tokyo's Rocket Gallery, Colette in Paris, and the Apartment in New York. In spring 2001, eight of these products were selected to be produced as a commercial line, three of which are featured in this exhibition: *do hit* (Marjin van der Poll), *do break* (Frank Tjepkema and Peter van der Jagt), and *do swing* (Thomas Bernstrand).

DUNNE & RABY

Founded 1994; based in London, England
Anthony Dunne
Born 1964, London, England
Fiona Raby
Born 1963, Singapore

Anthony Dunne and Fiona Raby, hailed by critic Rick Poynor as "two of Britain's most original and speculative design thinkers," explore the relationship between products and their social effects on owners and the public at large. Over the last decade they have concentrated their investigations on what they term "Hertzian space," the invisible electromagnetic spectrum emitted by all electronic goods. Dunne and Raby examine the by-products—the social and environmental implications as well as the unintended or unofficial uses— of these objects, revealing what they refer to as the "secret life of electronic products." They argue for a form of design that is more critical and speculative, less formally and commercially driven. In this vein, they initiate projects in which works are created to probe certain issues and values. Although not intended for the commercial market, one of the *Placebo* objects, *Compass Table*, was recently put into production by Hidden, a Dutch company. Dunne, an industrial designer by training, and Raby, an architect, lead the Critical Design Unit and serve as Senior Research Fellows in Computer-Related Design at the Royal College of Art in London. Their book *Design Noir: The Secret Life of Electronic Objects* (2001) is a continuation of their approach to design first outlined in *Hertzian Tales* (1999). Their work has appeared in solo exhibitions that include *Hertzian Tales* (1998), Air de Paris, and *Weeds, Aliens and Other Stories* (with Michael Anastassiades) (1998–2000), Habitat Pont Neuf, Paris. Group exhibitions include *Mind the Gap* (1999), Haus der Kulturen der Welt, Berlin; *Stealing Beauty* (1999), Institute of Contemporary Arts, London; *Continuum 001* (2000), Centre for Contemporary Art, Glasgow; *Inside Out* (2000), Design Museum, London; and *La Ville, le Gardin, la Memoire* (2000), Academie de France, Rome.

ELEPHANT DESIGN
Founded 1997; based in Tokyo, Japan
elephant design inverts conventional notions of product development by soliciting ideas for new products from the Japanese

public. Kohei Nishiyama founded elephant design and created a Web site, www .cuusoo.com, which bridges consumer, designer, and manufacturer in a novel way. Rather than making and then advertising a product, the site enables consumers to suggest items they would like to purchase as well as post proposals from designers. After careful evaluation of their manufacturing potential, the ideas are presented as virtual prototypes on the site and will be manufactured when the number of orders is sufficient to meet the cost of the production run. Since December 1999, several designs have been made and sold, including a number of sleek computer monitors. In 2001, sixty-seven prototypes awaited the minimum number of orders, and more than 7,000 ideas had been suggested by consumers. Among elephant design's offerings are a bed warmer, a mobile phone case, multipurpose plain metal cases to house electronic devices, and a translucent washing machine shaped like a doughnut that doubles as seating. Also on offer is *Insipid Collection* (2000), which reworks typical consumer products such as the telephone, fax machine, rice cooker, and vacuum cleaner by stripping them of superfluous details, leaving a minimal, ghostly white shell to express the objects' functionality. Continuing to circumvent convention, *Insipid* offers consumers archetypal forms rather than branded products.

MORENO FERRARI
Born 1952, La Spezia, Italy
Revolutionizing sportswear since 1975, C.P. Company incorporates the practicality and flexibility of uniforms and work attire

into its line of innovative clothing. In the early 1990s, C.P. Company founders Carlo and Sabina Rivetti discovered the work of fashion and interior designer Moreno Ferrari, who since 1994 has designed the men's and women's collections. Because the company has an interest in researching new materials and manufacturing techniques, Ferrari was encouraged to experiment and created some of his trademark pieces, including *Urban Protection* (1998–1999) and *Transformables* (2000), collections of adaptive clothing. Ferrari's designs are more akin to poetry than fashion styling, a by-product of his education in philosophy, his interests in the human condition, and his keen observations of urban life. He is inspired by events such as the G8 Summit in Genoa, Italy, with its mix of police and riot gear and the antiglobalization protestors' improvised protective wear, as well as the condition of refugees, the homeless, and cosmopolitan nomads. Ferrari's tailored and ingeniously engineered capes, raincoats, and parkas can be transformed into tents, kites, hammocks, and armchairs; jackets outfitted with smog masks, earphones, and personal alarms become tools for bodily protection and individual mobility. Ferrari's designs have garnered international acclaim by advancing the notion of clothing the body beyond the conventional ensemble and by looking toward re-envisioning fashion altogether.

DOUG GAROFALO

Born 1958, Schenectady, New York

Doug Garofalo established his studio, Garofalo Architects, in Chicago in 1992. His firm is known for producing experimental work through projects, research, and teaching, building connections between the theoretical and the practical. The practice works to "translate the fluidity, flexibility, and complexity of contemporary technologies into built form." Known for turning conventional suburban split-levels into dynamic dwelling spaces, Garofalo Architects has earned a decade's worth of accolades. Recently the firm was recognized as part of "The New Vanguard" in *Architectural Record* and included in the Emerging Voices program at the Architectural League of New York. Among Garofalo Architects' many projects are the *Derman Residence* (1992), Skokie, Illinois; *Thornton-Tomasetti Engineers Offices* (1999), Chicago; and, through an electronic collaboration with Greg Lynn Form (Hoboken, New Jersey) and McInturf Architects (Cincinnati, Ohio), the *Korean Presbyterian Church of New York* (1999), Queens, for which the team was awarded a Progressive Architects Citation. In addition to participating in various exhibitions across the United States, Garofalo is currently the facilitator at the Chicago-based design laboratory Archeworks, a nonprofit organization that pairs design practices with need-based areas. He has continued to be actively involved in both architecture and academia. He received his master's degree in architecture from Yale University in 1987 and is an associate professor in the School of Architecture at the University of Illinois, Chicago.

MARKKU HEDMAN

Born 1966, Espoo, Finland

Originally founded in 1997 as an architects' cooperative, Markku Hedman's practice has recently been reshaped into his singular venture, Architects MH. The company is concerned with the intersection of ecology and urban planning and is unified by a shared belief in a human responsibility to exist in solidarity with nature. This commitment is realized in projects for "mobile dwelling, open building, sustainable development, and integration of media." In Finland, a country where the preservation and integration of nature and contemporary lifestyles are interrelated, many of Hedman's architectural designs reaffirm this position. With *Kesä-Kontti (Summer Container)* (2001), for example, Hedman re-creates the traditional timber-framed holiday cabin as a transportable structure that is powered either by solar panels or a wind generator. Other dwelling projects, such as *Etana (Snail)* (2003), also aim for nominal environmental impact. Its main structure, like a snail's shell, can be easily relocated and contains an inflatable, transparent, insulating skin that expands to create additional space. *Snail* blends working and living spaces, providing a shelter that accommodates the owner's lifestyle. Hedman is currently pursuing a doctoral degree in architecture from Helsinki University of Technology and has completed postgraduate work at the University of Industrial Arts in Helsinki. He has won various national and international awards, including first prize in a competition for ecological housing in Viikki, Finland, and second prize in Vision 2025, an international competition held in Södermanland, Sweden (1994).

KOERS, ZEINSTRA, VAN GELDEREN
Founded 1996; based in Amsterdam, the Netherlands
Mikel van Gelderen
Born 1963, Den Bosch, the Netherlands
Ira Koers
Born 1970, Amsterdam, the Netherlands
Jurjen Zeinstra
Born 1961, Leeuwarden, the Netherlands
From large-scale urban planning to a small garden structure, Koers, Zeinstra, van Gelderen works at a variety of scales. Trained as architects, the members of this trio formed their partnership in 1996. Ira Koers, an architectural designer, is a graduate of Amsterdam's Rietveld Academy of Arts. Her two counterparts, Jurjen Zeinstra and Mikel van Gelderen, graduated from Delft's Technical University, Department of Architecture. Together they have been involved in many competitions and projects. In 1996, for example, Koers, Zeinstra, van Gelderen's plan for two hundred-plus dwellings in the Dutch city of Emmen was awarded first prize at Europan 4. Through an innovative interweaving of green and living spaces, the trio put a new spin on the urban oasis. Two years later, they received the Charlotte Köhler Prize, a prestigious Dutch award for young artists, for their inventive garden structure, *Tumble House* (1998). Interested in working out solutions to the noise and chaos of high-density living, they have been involved in various projects in and around Amsterdam. These include multiuse structures such as *Windows 80* (1998/2001), a student dormitory with commercial shops in Almere, and *Wester IJ-Dock* in Amsterdam,

a housing and office complex built over the water. Occasionally working in collaboration with other architects, the firm has been involved in research projects such as a 1998 typological study investigating living in noise-polluted areas. Zeinstra and van Gelderen have also been teaching periodically at their alma mater.

LOT-EK
Founded 1992; based in New York City
Giuseppe Lignano
Born 1963, Naples, Italy
Ada Tolla
Born 1964, Naples, Italy
After receiving degrees in architecture at the University of Naples, Ada Tolla and Giuseppe Lignano were awarded research fellowships at Columbia University in 1990–1991. The two decided to remain in New York City and in 1992 opened their own architecture studio, where they continue to specialize in the unconventional adaptations of familiar, man-made objects. LOT-EK's working method creatively reuses existing industrial objects, often merging technology with urban detritus. Its rapidly growing repertoire includes the *Morton Duplex* (1999), which repurposes a petroleum trailer tank to form a sleeping loft and bathrooms; *Mixer Project* (2000), a multimedia capsule created inside a suspended cement mixer; a parking ramp transformed into the new Sara Meltzer Gallery in New York (2000); and *TV-LITEs* (1997), eviscerated TV sets made into light fixtures. LOT-EK's unbuilt projects include the *Goree Memorial and Museum* (1997), a slave trade and navigation memorial and museum in Senegal comprised of ship-ping containers; a proposal to transform a section of fuselage from a 747 airplane into a student pavilion for the University of Washington; and a skateboard park made from a steel water tank. The studio's projects have been exhibited at the Museum of Modern Art and the Whitney Museum of American Art, New York; the *Venice Architectural Biennale*; Vitra Design Museum, Weil am Rhein, Germany; and the San Francisco Museum of Modern Art. Pushing the boundaries of convention, LOT-EK's work intelligently challenges distinctions between aesthetics and functionality, creatively blurs the categories of architecture and art, and critically explores the possibilities of technology and media.

MVRDV
Founded 1991; based in Rotterdam, the Netherlands
Winy Maas
Born 1959, Schijndel, the Netherlands
Jacob van Rijs
Born 1964, Amsterdam, the Netherlands
Nathalie de Vries
Born 1965, Appingedam, the Netherlands
In 1991, Winy Maas, Jacob van Rijs, and Nathalie de Vries established their office for architecture, urbanism, and landscape design in Rotterdam. In little more than a decade, these 1990 graduates of Delft's Technical University have become one of the Netherlands' leading architectural practices, garnering international acclaim for their diverse and innovative projects. Past works include the *WoZoCos* (1997), an apartment complex for some of Amsterdam's elderly, for which the firm received the Merkelbach Award from the Amsterdam Fund for the Arts (1997), the

J. A. van Eck Prize from the Dutch Architects Association (2000), and finalist status for the VI Mies van der Rohe Award for European Architecture (1999); and *Villa VPRO* (1997), the headquarters for one of the Netherlands' largest television companies. Recent work includes *Dutch Pavilion* (2000) at *Expo 2000* in Hanover, Germany, which was nominated for the European Union Prize for Contemporary Architecture and the World Architecture Awards; *Housing Silo* (2002), a mixed-use structure of private residences and commercial spaces built off a pier in Amsterdam; and the Hageneiland Housing development (2001) that utilizes different cladding materials—wood, stone, tile, metal—to produce a differentiated, village-like community, which received the Netherlands Architecture Institute Prize (2002). MVRDV pursues its methodological research on density through projects such as *MetaCity/ DataTown* (1998), which creates a virtualized space from vast data inputs about growth and waste; *Pig City* (2000), an animation that explores ecological meat production; and the book *FARMAX* (1998).

NUCLEO
Founded 1997; based in Turin, Italy
Nucleo is a group of designers with mutual interests who formed a partnership soon after meeting at the European Design Institute in Turin. Trained as industrial designers, they see their company as an eclectic, conceptually oriented team. What sets it apart from other firms is the scope of its interests, which follow an object from early conceptual stages through its packaging and advertising all the way to the user-object relationship. By designing the various phases of an object's life, Nucleo's aim is to place the user at the center of its designs. Because the team is interested in design as a cultural element and the emotional relationships it can foster, its products move beyond mere utility. *Terra: The Grass Arm-chair* (2000), exemplifies the group's creative process. Dependent on the user, the chair must be "grown," simultaneously dematerializing and re-materializing over time. *Terra* was among the selections for the prestigious Compasso D'Oro Prize in 2001. An event designed by Nucleo for the 2001 Salon Satellite in Milan explored water as a metaphor for consumerism, offering visitors an array of ephemeral products—chairs, lights, trays—all made from ice. As Nucleo states: "The durability of a product is almost always more than the life we allow it."

OFFICE OF MOBILE DESIGN (OMD)
Founded 1998; based in Los Angeles, California
Jennifer Siegal
Born 1965, New York City
Headed by Jennifer Siegal, the Office of Mobile Design (OMD) is dedicated to developing a variety of non-permanently sited structures. For OMD, a mobile structure must be flexible and demountable so that it can be moved from location to location. The range of solutions designed by OMD include *Portable House* (2001) a prefabricated home; the *Portable Construction Training Center* (1998); *Mobile ECO Lab* (1998), used to teach children about environmental issues; and *PuppetMobile* (2002), a traveling theater and classroom for CalArts' Cotsen Center

for Puppetry and the Arts in Valencia, California. OMD was recently commissioned to design a sustainable development of more than forty portable and stackable housing units in downtown Los Angeles. Whether a mobile home or a classroom, each OMD design is uniquely suited to the changing environments of nomadic lifestyles. Siegal, who holds a master's degree in architecture from the Southern California Institute of Architecture (SCI-Arc) in Los Angeles, professes the importance of community in her designs. She teaches architecture at Woodbury University in California and was a Loeb Fellow at Harvard University's Graduate School of Design (2002–2003), where she explored urban community-based practices and investigated the use of intelligent, kinetic, and lightweight materials. She is the editor of *Mobile: The Art of Portable Architecture* (2002), a survey of contemporary approaches. From challenging the stereotypes of trailer homes to rethinking the biases against transience, Siegal upholds the idea of a dynamic, accessible, and sustainable architecture, something missing in the stationary sprawl and generic clutter of the landscape.

R&SIE...
Founded 1989; based in Paris, France
Stéphanie Lavaux
Born 1966, Saint-Denis, Réunion
François Roche
Born 1961, Paris, France
François Roche and Stéphanie Lavaux, principals at R&Sie..., approach architecture–both the practice and the discipline–as a critical tool. Seeking to create a dialogue between project and

landscape, they let two precepts undergird their work: "hyperlocalism" and "freak hybridizations." When working on a design, they take into consideration the existing site, closely scrutinizing the land and locale in order to best integrate their project, and often utilize warping and morphing technologies to create new interventions and modifications to the terrain. *(Un)Plug* (2000/2001) is a Parisian office-building proposal, commissioned by the research department of the French Public Electricity Company, designed for the self-sufficient use of energy. By wrapping the building in materials made of thermal sensors, R&Sie... conceived of the facade as a skin to absorb the sun's energy. *Maison Barak* (2002), a residence near Montpellier, France, employs a green, polyurethane, tentlike surface to disguise a cement-block structure beneath. The shape and color of this "skin" mimic the surrounding terrain, thereby camouflaging its appearance in order to satisfy the region's restrictive building codes. Other recent projects include *Wire Frame* (2002), a bridge structure comprised of a web of wires designed in collaboration with artist Philippe Parreno and built over the Burgundy channel, which houses a walkway and restaurant; and *Silverelief/B-mu* (2002), a proposal for a new museum of contemporary art in Bangkok, Thailand, which creates an interplay between airborne particulates and the luminosity of the city's atmosphere. The work of R&Sie... has been exhibited widely at venues that include the Pompidou Center, Paris (2003); the Institute of Contemporary Arts, London (2002); ZKM Karlsruhe, Germany (2001); and the Storefront for Art and Architecture, New York (2001).

MARTÍN RUIZ DE AZÚA
Born 1965, Vitoria, Spain

Martín Ruiz de Azúa graduated from Barcelona University in 1995 with a degree in the fine arts with a special concentration in design, and received his master's degree in architecture and exhibition design from Barcelona Polytechnic. His works share a concern for individual freedom and reflect on the most fundamental or basic human needs. In this spirit he proposed changing the Red Cross, a symbol of humanitarian aid, to an equal sign, emphasizing the desire for social justice. His *Human Chair* (2002), as the name implies, is a seating solution created for and by a group of people who form a circle and must simultaneously sit down using each other's knees as a seat. People's dependence on each other can also be seen in *Interaction* (2001), two inflatable cushions that are connected, thereby transmitting any movements made to each person. *Basic House* (2000), an inflatable shelter that can be carried in one's pocket, is designed for the minimalist nomads of the future and will be "anticonsumerist, aimless, virtual, and omnicultural," he says. Ruiz de Azúa received the City of Barcelona Prize for design in 2000 and has since received the Expo Hogar Regalo Award four times. He freelances as a designer and teaches the history of design at the Elisava School in Barcelona.

ALEJANDRO STÖBERL
Born 1963, Buenos Aires, Argentina

Trained as an architect at Belgrano University in Buenos Aires, Stöberl worked at CMA Design Studio in New York City from 1990 to 1992. Returning to Argentina in 1993, he accepted a faculty position at Buenos Aires National University and opened his own architecture practice. Stöberl's recent projects include developing prototypical houses designed to keep costs low and construction productivity high through the use of prefabricated elements that are easily transported and quickly erected. Such works include *Prefabricated Wooden House* (2001), a sixty-square-meter glass box with a series of wooden louvers, and *Prefabricated Concrete House* (2002), a sixty-six-square-meter structure forming an extended concrete shed whose moveable panels connect inside to outside. Both designs offer an affordable and flexible solution in an expensive housing market. Stöberl is the recipient of numerous awards, including first prize at Buenos Aires' biennial of architecture (1997), second prize at the Shinkenchiku Membrane Design Competition (Tokyo, 1997), Best House of the Year (1997) from Diario El Cronista Comercial, and the Roca Prize for Best Design (2000). His work has been published internationally and has been featured at the biennial of architecture in São Paulo (2000) and Buenos Aires (1997) and in the exhibitions *16 Expresiones sobre 2* (1999), *10 x 50 Terreno de Arquitectura* (2000), and *Tecnología y Arquitectura* (2001) at the Museo de Arte Moderno in Buenos Aires.

SU11 ARCHITECTURE+DESIGN
Founded 1998; based in New York City
Ferda Kolatan
Born 1966, Cologne, Germany
Erich Schoenenberger
Born 1966, St. Gallen, Switzerland
Ferda Kolatan and Erich Schoenenberger formed su11 as a platform to explore an experimental approach to architecture and design. While in New York City attending Columbia University's famed "paperless design studios," which pioneered the use of digital technologies in architecture, Kolatan and Schoenenberger began to think about ways to make design and architecture more "user-friendly and adaptable." From 1995–2000, Kolatan worked as senior designer for the architectural firm of Smith-Miller+Hawkinson in New York. Schoenenberger worked for Santiago Calatrava in Zürich and in New York as senior designer for Kol/Mac Studio. After three years of loose collaboration, they left their respective firms and founded su11. The name stands for the founding date, Sunday the eleventh – like their practice, the name is open and essentially undefined, available for reinterpretation and reinvention. Making the most of new technologies, materials, and products, the studio's approach emphasizes the "mutual connectivity of different design types, methods, and media." In projects such as *Composite Housing* (2002), su11 conceives of architecture as modular, breaking down these modules into units that can be exchanged, updated, and reconfigured as needed. The studio's projects have been widely published and exhibited internationally, including *ART Basel* in Switzerland (2001) and *Archilab*

2001 in Orléans, France. They received the 2001 International Contemporary Furniture Fair Editor's Award for best new designers.

SHIGERU UCHIDA
Born 1943, Yokohama, Japan
Shigeru Uchida is a principal member of the influential firm Studio 80, which he founded in 1981 with Toru Nishioka and Ikuyo Mitsuhashi. This Tokyo-based architect looks to Japanese history and spiritual traditions for inspiration, but his designs have a distinctly modern approach. Involved in a wide range of projects, from interiors and furniture to urban planning, he is perhaps best known for the fashion boutiques he designed for Yohji Yamamoto, Issey Miyake, and Junko Shimada; the Hotel Il Palazzo with Aldo Rossi (1989); the Kobe Fashion Museum (1993); and a range of cabinets and furniture. Believing that "the purpose of design in everyday life is to support the life of real people," Uchida reinforces his highly functional works with spiritual undertones, as in his *Paper Tea Houses* (1993–2001). His work is included in the collections of the Metropolitan Museum of Art, New York, the San Francisco Museum of Modern Art, and the Musée des Arts Decoratifs de Montréal. Uchida has also been recognized through awards given for his innovations in design, including the Japan Interior Designers Association Award (1981), the Mainichi Design Award (1987), and the First Kuwasawa Design Award (1993). He graduated from Kuwasawa Design School in Tokyo in 1966, where he later became a lecturer from 1974–1978 after establishing Uchida Design Studio in 1970.

PAOLO ULIAN

Born 1961, Massa, Italy

Overwhelmed by the waste and the plethora of goods in the marketplace, Paolo Ulian is dedicated to turning discarded objects into useful products. Trained in Florence as an industrial designer, Ulian attributes his ecological conscience to the time he spent in Carrara, Italy, a city known for its high-quality marble and where he has chosen to practice. After an assistantship with designer Enzo Mari in Milan (1990–1992), his design motivation and method began to crystallize, and he pursued a trajectory that marries design with environmental responsibility. In the 1990s, after he learned that roughly seventy percent of quarried marble was wasted and eventually ground into powder, he began to use remnants from the quarries to design products such as a bowl whose curvature relies on the dynamite holes found in scrap marble. Working with refuse, he recycles and reuses, creating innovative and often poetic objects for everyday use. He presented his *Screen Onda*, made of discarded corrugated pinewood, at the Opos showroom in 1994. In 1998, he and his brother, Giuseppe, designed a line of products from industrial wood scraps. His inventiveness can also be seen in the multifunctional *Cabriolet/Occasional Table* (2000), a combination storage table and seating unit, or the *Pane e Salame Knife* (1999), also designed with his brother, that combines two blades for bread and for meat in one utensil. Ulian's work also displays a humorous side, which is evident in *Mat Walk* (2002), a bath mat with built-in slippers designed for the *Hotel*

Droog installation at the 2000 International Furniture Fair in Milan, or in his *Greediness Meter* (2002), a ruler made of chocolate. He has been the recipient of various honors, including being named Design Talent of the Year by *Design Report* (2000).

MAREK WALCZAK, MICHAEL MCALLISTER, JAKUB SEGEN, AND PETER KENNARD

Marek Walczak
Born 1957, London, England
Michael McAllister
Born 1955, Havre de Grace, Maryland
Jakub Segen
Born 1947, Wrocław, Poland
Peter Kennard
Born 1955, Washington, D.C.

The four-member design team for *Dialog* came together under organizer Marek Walczak, who was educated at the Architectural Association, London, and Cooper Union, New York. His work is an extended study of the repercussions of technology on space as evidenced in his innovative projects involving architecture and new media: *Apartment* (2001) with Martin Wattenberg, in which ideas of common speech are translated into spatial projections; and *Adrift* (2002), an online collaboration with writer Helen Thorington and musician Jesse Gilbert. In 2000, the Walker commissioned *WonderWalker*, and Walczak again teamed with Wattenberg to design this digital update of the seventeenth-century *wunderkammer*, which enables users to create their own online collection of Internet curiosities (wonderwalker.walkerart.org). For *Dialog*, Walczak and a former student at the University of the Arts, Philadelphia,

Michael McAllister, designed the project's physical and conceptual architecture. McAllister shares Walczak's interest in human and computer interactions. Individually, his work has explored the possibilities of sustaining natural and fallible human processes alongside precise, digital technologies. He brought his expertise and experience in the field of furniture design to the project, while Jakub Segen, who holds a doctorate in electrical and bioengineering from Carnegie-Mellon University in Pittsburgh, developed gesture recognition software. This allows for *Dialog*'s multiple-touch interface, which is also being used on the public facade of the renovated 7 World Trade Center in New York. A veteran in the field of real-time interactive graphics, Peter Kennard served as the programmer on this project while continuing his own work on interactive architectural media installations.

MARCEL WANDERS
Born 1963, Boxtel, the Netherlands

An influential figure in Dutch design since the mid-1980s, Marcel Wanders continues to astonish with his shape-shifting ideas and award-winning projects. His engaging and memorable works reinvent meaning in ordinary objects whose uncanny forms, materials, and functions resonate within the familiar. As Yvònne G.J.M. Joris has written, "Wanders Wonders is not about inventing the wheel but about the wheel of invention." His *Knotted Chair* (1996) is literally made from knotted rope, and though strengthened with epoxy, its gravity-defying form gives pause. His sense of whimsy is evi-

dent in the shape of his porcelain *Egg Vases* (1997), for example, which were formed by stuffing latex condoms with hard-boiled eggs, or in *Set-Up Shades* (1988), a lamp made from stacked lampshades. Having sold the Wanders Wonders label to Casper Cissers, Amsterdam-based Wanders is presently maintaining the Marcel Wanders Studio and serving as art director for the pioneering design firm Moooi, whose name is derived from the Dutch word for beautiful. Hoping to lead Moooi toward independent recognition, Wanders would like to see the company produce unusual projects by other designers, including some that might otherwise go unmade.

ALLAN WEXLER
Born 1949, Bridgeport, Connecticut

New York–based Allan Wexler is an artist who makes utensils, furniture, and structures. His provocative body of work, spanning more than thirty years, is comprised of studies and experiments in modes of building and design—meditations on form and function. Though he studied architecture, receiving his undergraduate degree from the Rhode Island School of Design in Providence and his master's degree from Pratt Institute, New York, Wexler does not consider himself an architect. Once, after watching a potter throw a pot, he was inspired to try his hand at "throwing a building." This moment sparked his artistic trajectory, from which three major strains have emerged: a preoccupation with the creative process; an interest in daily rituals; and an exploration of nature's impact on architecture. In all instances, self-generated and existing constraints that enable accidents and discoveries are important to Wexler. For example, while creating his *Temple Houses* series (1977–1978), he limited his materials to one-by-eight-inch pine boards, a saw, hammer, and nails. He added the element of time to his working equation with *Chair a Day* (1985), a sixteen-day project in which he spent eight hours creating each chair, using preestablished materials, tools, and dimensions. Other projects, such as *Crate House* (1991) and *Parson's Kitchen* (1994) (commissioned by New York's Parsons School of Design), collapse domestic space into small, fully functional, moveable components. Wexler's large and diverse body of work has been exhibited internationally for more than two decades with solo exhibitions at the San Francisco Museum of Modern Art; Stadtgalerie Saarbrucken, Germany; the Maryland Institute College of Art, Baltimore; Karl Ernst Osthaus-Museum, Germany; DeCordova Museum, Lincoln, Nebraska; the Forum Gallery, St. Louis, Missouri; San Diego Museum of Contemporary Art; Jewish Museum, New York; and the Institute of Contemporary Art, Philadelphia. His work was the subject of the book and exhibition *Custom Built: A Twenty-Year Survey of Work by Allan Wexler* (1998).

RACHEL WHITEREAD
Born 1963, London, England
Visual artist Rachel Whiteread is best known for her sculptures and installations created by casting spaces and environments – either interior spaces or exterior elements. Her practice is akin to the pho-

tographic process, in which an imprint becomes a record or document that represents objects in a symbolic manner. The casts vary between representations of negative and positive space, often evoking ideas of absence and loss. In the 1990s, Whiteread emerged from England among a new generation of young British artists, but quickly earned individual acclaim through the Tate Gallery's famed Turner Prize in 1993 and a medal at the 1997 *Venice Biennale*. Her landmark work, *House* (1993–1994), was a cast made of the interior space of a condemned Victorian terrace house in London. It remained in the building's place after its demolition, a solitary reminder of the city's past, but public and media controversy eventually led to its destruction. Her first project in the United States was the translucent cast-resin sculpture *Watertower* (1998), a public art installation commissioned by New York City's Public Art Fund, which focused on one of Manhattan's architectural icons installed on a rooftop in the heart of the Soho community. *Daybed* (1999) is a continuation of her sculptural work, but in an unusual mode of practice – furniture design. She worked in collaboration with the British manufacturer SCP to produce *Daybed* based on a series of related sculptures. It was first presented in the SCP-sponsored *Please Touch* exhibition displayed at the Lighthouse in Glasgow in 1999. In the summer of 2001 in London, the Serpentine Gallery held a retrospective of Whiteread's work, and her public art commission, *Monument*, was installed in Trafalgar Square.

WWW.FORTUNECOOKIES.DK
Founded 1998; based in Øksnehallen, Denmark

Looking for a new approach to fashion design, fortunecookies stripped its product down to an essential unit, the "building block." Interested in narrowing the gap between the necessary standardization of the mass-produced object and the consumer's desire for individuality, fortunecookies produced squares of felt that rely upon consumers to complete the design process by configuring and recon-figuring their own clothing. The firm's aim is twofold: to create an identity for the building block, enabling it to stand on its own with a brandlike identity; and to allow consumers to shape their own identity through the product. Reinforcing the importance of the consumer cum designer, fortunecookies held workshops in which these designs were shown, and several were selected for exhibition. The studio was founded by Christina Widholm, fash-ion designer; Jacob Ravn, furniture and graphic designer; Stine Andersen, textile designer; and Jonas Larsen, ceramic and glass artist. The firm's departure from ready-to-wear has earned it a place in an international array of publications, includ-ing *I.D. Magazine* (2000), *Forum* (1999), and *Politiken* (1998).

EXHIBITION CHECKLIST

1. **Michael Anastassiades**
   Anti-Social Light 2001
   acrylic on resin, light fittings,
   electronics
   21 ⅞ x 7 ⅞ x 7 ⅞ in.
   55.5 x 20 x 20 cm
   Courtesy Michael Anastassiades,
   London

2. **Atelier Bow-Wow**
   Moth House 2000
   wood, plexiglass
   7 ⅞ x 25 ⁹⁄₁₆ x 31 ½ in. model
   20 x 65 x 80 cm
   Courtesy Atelier Bow-Wow, Tokyo

3. **Atelier Bow-Wow**
   Moth House 2000
   DVD
   Courtesy Atelier Bow-Wow, Tokyo

4. **Shigeru Ban**
   Paper Loghouse 1995
   cardboard tubes, plastic crates,
   canvas, wood
   138 x 160 x 160 in.
   350.52 x 406.4 x 406.4 cm
   Courtesy Shigeru Ban, Tokyo

5. **Jop van Bennekom**
   *RE– #1: The Home Issue "Living
   Apart Together"* spring 1997
   offset lithograph on paper
   11 ⅞ x 8 ⁷⁄₁₆ x ³⁄₁₆ in.
   30.16 x 21.43 x .48 cm
   Private collection, Minneapolis

6. **Jop van Bennekom**
   *RE– #1: The Home Issue "Living Apart
   Together"* with insert *RE– #1.5: A Special
   Issue "Streetwise"* spring 1997
   offset lithograph on paper
   11 ⅞ x 8 ⁷⁄₁₆ x ³⁄₁₆ in.
   30.16 x 21.43 x .48 cm
   Private collection, Minneapolis

7. **Jop van Bennekom**
RE– #2: The Media Issue "Inbetween Media and Daily Life"   February 1998
offset lithograph on paper
11 ⅞ x 8 3/16 x ⅛ in.
30.16 x 20.8 x .32 cm
Courtesy Jop van Bennekom, Amsterdam

8. **Jop van Bennekom**
RE– #2: The Media Issue "Inbetween Media and Daily Life"   February 1998
offset lithograph on paper
11 ⅞ x 8 3/16 x ⅛ in.
30.16 x 20.8 x .32 cm
Private collection, Minneapolis

9–11. **Jop van Bennekom**
RE– #3: The Sex Issue "On Sex"
August 1998
offset lithograph on paper
11 ⅞ x 8 ¼ x ⅛ in.
30.16 x 20.96 x .32 cm
Courtesy Jop van Bennekom, Amsterdam

12. **Jop van Bennekom**
RE– Magazine #4: Boring!   May 2000
offset lithograph on paper
11 ¾ x 8 ⅝ x ¼ in.
29.85 x 21.91 x .64 cm
Courtesy Jop van Bennekom, Amsterdam

13. **Jop van Bennekom**
RE– Magazine #4: Boring!   May 2000
offset lithograph on paper
11 ¾ x 8 ⅝ x ¼ in.
29.85 x 21.91 x .64 cm
Private collection, Minneapolis

14–15. **Jop van Bennekom**
RE– Magazine #5: The Anti-attitude Issue "Re-connect yourself!"   November 2000
offset lithograph on paper
8 11/16 x 11 11/16 x ¼ in.
22 x 29.7 x .64 cm
Courtesy Jop van Bennekom, Amsterdam

16–17. **Jop van Bennekom**
RE– Magazine #6: The Manic Issue "The Information Trashcan"
March 2001
offset lithograph on paper
11 11/16 x 8 11/16 x 3/16 in.
29.69 x 22.07 x .48 cm
Courtesy Jop van Bennekom, Amsterdam

18–19. **Jop van Bennekom**
RE– Magazine #7: Re-View
September 2001
offset lithograph on paper
11 ⅝ x 8 ⅞ x 5/16 in.
29.53 x 22.54 x .79 cm
Courtesy Jop van Bennekom, Amsterdam

20–21. **Jop van Bennekom**
RE– Magazine #23: It's Spring Two Thousand Seven (2007)
February 2002
offset lithograph on paper, rubber band
11 11/16 x 8 ⅞ x ¼ in.
29.69 x 22.54 x .64 cm
Courtesy Jop van Bennekom, Amsterdam

* Shown at the Walker Art Center only

22. **Thomas Bernstrand**
    do swing 2001
    stainless steel, lamp fittings, shades
    17 ⁵⁄₁₆ x 12 ³⁄₁₆ x 4 in.
    44 x 31 x 10.16 cm
    Courtesy do create, Amsterdam

23. **Jurgen Bey**
    Kokon Chair 1997–1999
    wooden chair, synthetic elastic
    fiber coating
    31½ x 39⅜ x 18⅞ in.
    80 x 100 x 48 cm
    Courtesy Jurgen Bey, Rotterdam

24. **Blu Dot**
    Free Play 2003
    high density polyethylene, steel, magnets
    12 x 120 x 14 in. variable
    30.48 x 304.8 x 35.56 cm variable
    Courtesy Blu Dot (Maurice Blanks, John
    Christakos, Charles Lazor), Minneapolis

25. **Julian Lion Boxenbaum**
    Rugelah Chair 2000
    wool felt, cotton and polyester
    fabric, steel, paint
    44 x 44 x 32 in.
    111.76 x 111.76 x 81.28 cm
    Courtesy Julian Lion Boxenbaum, Milan

26. **Constantin Boym**
    Upstate (Ellenville, NY) 2002
    china plate with digital printing
    12 x 12 x 1⅛ in.
    30.48 x 30.48 x 2.86 cm
    Courtesy Boym Partners Incorporated,
    New York

27. **Constantin Boym**
    Upstate (High Falls, NY) 2002
    china plate with digital printing
    12 x 12 x 1⅛ in.
    30.48 x 30.48 x 2.86 cm
    Courtesy Boym Partners Incorporated,
    New York

28. **Constantin Boym**
    Upstate (Kerhonkson, NY) 2002
    china plate with digital printing
    12 x 12 x 1⅛ in.
    30.48 x 30.48 x 2.86 cm
    Courtesy Boym Partners Incorporated,
    New York

29. **Constantin Boym**
    Upstate (Kippelbush, NY) 2002
    china plate with digital printing
    12 x 12 x 1⅛ in.
    30.48 x 30.48 x 2.86 cm
    Courtesy Boym Partners Incorporated,
    New York

30. **Constantin Boym**
    Upstate (Mohonk, NY) 2002
    china plate with digital printing
    12 x 12 x 1⅛ in.
    30.48 x 30.48 x 2.86 cm
    Courtesy Boym Partners Incorporated,
    New York

31. **Constantin Boym**
    Upstate (Pataukunk, NY) 2002
    china plate with digital printing
    12 x 12 x 1⅛ in.
    30.48 x 30.48 x 2.86 cm
    Courtesy Boym Partners Incorporated,
    New York

32. **Constantin Boym and Laurene
    Leon Boym**
    *Buildings of Disaster (Chernobyl, April 26,
    1986)* 1998–2001
    bonded nickel
    4 ⅞ x 2 ⅞ x 4 ⅛ in.
    12.38 x 7.3 x 10.48 cm
    Courtesy Boym Partners Incorporated,
    New York

33. **Constantin Boym and Laurene
    Leon Boym**
    *Buildings of Disaster (O.J. Car Chase,
    Los Angeles, June 17, 1994)* 1998–2001
    bonded nickel
    ⅞ x 6 ¾ x 1 ⅞ in.
    2.22 x 17.15 x 4.76 cm
    Courtesy Boym Partners Incorporated,
    New York

34. **Constantin Boym and Laurene
    Leon Boym**
    *Buildings of Disaster (Oklahoma City
    Federal Building, April 19, 1995)*
    1998–2001
    bonded nickel
    2 ⅝ x 3 ¼ x 3 ¼ in.
    6.67 x 8.26 x 8.26 cm
    Courtesy Boym Partners Incorporated,
    New York

35. **Constantin Boym and Laurene
    Leon Boym**
    *Buildings of Disaster (Texas School Book
    Depository, November 22, 1963)*
    1998–2001
    bonded nickel
    3 ⅛ x 4 ⅜ x 5 ¼ in.
    7.94 x 11.11 x 13.34 cm
    Courtesy Boym Partners Incorporated,
    New York

36. **Constantin Boym and Laurene
    Leon Boym**
    *Buildings of Disaster (The Pentagon,
    September 11, 2001)* 1998–2001
    bonded nickel
    ⅞ x 5 x 5 in.
    2.22 x 12.7 x 12.7 cm
    Courtesy Boym Partners Incorporated,
    New York

37. **Constantin Boym and Laurene
    Leon Boym**
    *Buildings of Disaster (The Unabomber's
    Cabin, 1997)* 1998–2001
    bonded nickel
    2 ⅜ x 2 ⅝ x 2 ¼ in.
    6.03 x 6.67 x 5.72 cm
    Courtesy Boym Partners Incorporated,
    New York

38. **Constantin Boym and Laurene
    Leon Boym**
    *Buildings of Disaster (The Watergate,
    June 17, 1972)* 1998–2001
    bonded nickel
    1 ¾ x 6 ⅝ x 3 ⅛ in.
    4.45 x 16.83 x 7.94 cm
    Courtesy Boym Partners Incorporated,
    New York

39. **Constantin Boym and Laurene
    Leon Boym**
    *Buildings of Disaster (The World Trade
    Center, February 26, 1993)* 1998–2001
    bonded nickel
    5 ⅝ x 2 ⅞ x 2 ½ in.
    14.29 x 7.3 x 6.35 cm
    Courtesy Boym Partners Incorporated,
    New York

* Shown at the Walker Art Center only

40. **Constantin Boym and Laurene Leon Boym**
Buildings of Disaster (The World Trade Center, September 11, 2001) 1998–2001
bonded nickel
5 ¾ x 3 x 2 ½ in.
14.61 x 7.62 x 6.35 cm
Courtesy Boym Partners Incorporated, New York

41. **Constantin Boym and Laurene Leon Boym**
Buildings of Disaster (Three Mile Island, March 28, 1979) 1998–2001
bonded nickel
2 ½ x 5 ½ x 3 ¼ in.
6.35 x 13.97 x 8.26 cm
Courtesy Boym Partners Incorporated, New York

42. **Constantin Boym and Laurene Leon Boym**
Buildings of Disaster (Triangle Shirtwaist Company, March 25, 1911) 1998–2001
bonded nickel
4 x 2 ¾ x 2 ¾ in.
10.16 x 6.99 x 6.99 cm
Courtesy Boym Partners Incorporated, New York

43. **Constantin Boym and Laurene Leon Boym**
Buildings of Disaster (Waco, Texas, April 19, 1993) 1998–2001
bonded nickel
2 x 5 ¼ x 2 ¼ in.
5.08 x 13.34 x 5.72 cm
Courtesy Boym Partners Incorporated, New York

44. **Constantin Boym and Laurene Leon Boym**
Buildings of Disaster (Texas A&M Bonfire, November 18, 1999) 1998–2001
bonded nickel
3 ⅝ x 3 x 3 in.
9.21 x 7.62 x 7.62 cm
Courtesy Boym Partners Incorporated, New York

45. **Constantin Boym and Laurene Leon Boym**
Buildings of Disaster (The Alma Tunnel, Paris, August 31, 1997) 2002
bonded nickel
1 ½ x 7 ⅛ x 1 ⅞ in.
3.81 x 18.1 x 4.76 cm
Courtesy Boym Partners Incorporated, New York

46. **Constantin Boym and Laurene Leon Boym**
Buildings of Disaster (The Dakota Building, December 8, 1980) 2002
bonded nickel
3 ⅞ x 3 ⅜ x 2 ⅞ in.
9.84 x 8.57 x 7.3 cm
Courtesy Boym Partners Incorporated, New York

*47. **Anthony Dunne and Fiona Raby**
Compass Table from *Placebo Project* 2001
MDF, 25 compasses
29 ½ x 29 ½ x 29 ½ in.
75 x 75 x 75 cm
Courtesy Dunne & Raby, London

*48. **Anthony Dunne and Fiona Raby**
Diane, Arabella and Compass Table 2001
photograph on aluminum
36 ¼ x 24 ⁷⁄₁₆ in.
92 x 62 cm
photographer: Jason Evans
Courtesy Dunne & Raby, London

*49. **Anthony Dunne and Fiona Raby**
Electricity Drain from *Placebo Project* 2001
MDF, stainless steel, electrical wire, plug
17 ¹¹⁄₁₆ x 17 ¹¹⁄₁₆ x 17 ¹¹⁄₁₆ in.
45 x 45 x 45 cm
Courtesy Dunne & Raby, London

*50. **Anthony Dunne and Fiona Raby**
Emma, Constance and Electricity Drain 2001
photograph on aluminum
36 ¼ x 24 ⁷⁄₁₆ in.
92 x 62 cm
photographer: Jason Evans
Courtesy Dunne & Raby, London

*51. **Anthony Dunne and Fiona Raby**
Electro-draught Excluder from *Placebo Project* 2001
MDF, antistatic foam
22 ⅝ x 20 ½ x 5 ⅛ in.
57.5 x 52 x 13 cm
Courtesy Dunne & Raby, London

*52. **Anthony Dunne and Fiona Raby**
Lauren and Electro-draught Excluder 2001
photograph on aluminum
36 ¼ x 24 ⁷⁄₁₆ in.
92 x 62 cm
photographer: Jason Evans
Courtesy Dunne & Raby, London

*53. **Anthony Dunne and Fiona Raby**
GPS Table from *Placebo Project* 2001
MDF, GPS unit and display
29 ½ x 23 ⅝ x 23 ⅝ in.
75 x 60 x 60 cm
Courtesy Dunne & Raby, London

*54. **Anthony Dunne and Fiona Raby**
Dick and GPS Table 2001
photograph on aluminum
36 ¼ x 24 ⁷⁄₁₆ in.
92 x 62 cm
photographer: Jason Evans
Courtesy Dunne & Raby, London

*55. **Anthony Dunne and Fiona Raby**
Loft from *Placebo Project* 2001
MDF, lead-lined box
93 ¾ x 31 ½ x 4 ⁷⁄₁₆ in.
238.2 x 80 x 11.2 cm
Courtesy Dunne & Raby, London

*56. **Anthony Dunne and Fiona Raby**
Sofie and Loft 2001
photograph on aluminum
36 ¼ x 24 ⁷⁄₁₆ in.
92 x 62 cm
photographer: Jason Evans
Courtesy Dunne & Raby, London

57. **Anthony Dunne and Fiona Raby**
Nipple Chair from *Placebo Project* 2001
MDF, electromagnetic sensors, motor
37 ⅜ x 17 ¹¹/₁₆ x 27 ³/₁₆ in.
95 x 45 x 69 cm
Courtesy Dunne & Raby, London

58. **Anthony Dunne and Fiona Raby**
Neil and Nipple Chair 2001
photograph on aluminum
36 ¼ x 24 ⁷/₁₆ in.
92 x 62 cm
photographer: Jason Evans
Courtesy Dunne & Raby, London

*59. **Anthony Dunne and Fiona Raby**
Phone Table from *Placebo Project* 2001
MDF, electromagnetic sensor, electro-
luminescent flat light
43 ⁵/₁₆ x 9 ¹/₁₆ x 12 ¹/₁₆ in.
110 x 22.9 x 30.5 cm
Courtesy Dunne & Raby, London

*60. **Anthony Dunne and Fiona Raby**
Tracey and Phone Table 2001
photograph on aluminum
36 ¼ x 24 ⁷/₁₆ in.
92 x 62 cm
photographer: Jason Evans
Courtesy Dunne & Raby, London

61. **elephant design**
Cordless Phone from *Insipid Collection*
2000
Corian, electronics
1 ⁹/₁₆ x 8 ¼ x 8 ¼ in.
4 x 21 x 21 cm
Courtesy elephant design co. ltd., Tokyo

62. **elephant design**
Rice Cooker from *Insipid Collection* 2000
Corian, electronics
8 ¼ x 9 ¹³/₁₆ x 9 ⁷/₁₆ in.
21 x 25 x 24 cm
Courtesy Makoto Miyazaki

63. **elephant design**
Paper Circulator from *Insipid Collection*
2002
paper, aluminum, electronics
70 ⅞ x 19 ¹¹/₁₆ x 19 ¹¹/₁₆ in.
180 x 50 x 50 cm
Courtesy Takeo Company, Japan

64. **elephant design**
Microwave Oven from *Insipid Collection*
2000
Corian, electronics
11 ¼ x 14 ⁷/₁₆ x 18 ⁵/₁₆ in.
28.5 x 36.7 x 46.5 cm
Courtesy Makoto Miyazaki

65. **elephant design**
Refrigerator from *Insipid Collection*
2000
Corian, electronics
21 ¹/₁₆ x 19 ¹¹/₁₆ x 19 ½ in.
53.5 x 50 x 49.5 cm
Courtesy elephant design co. ltd., Tokyo

66-67. **Moreno Ferrari**
Kite from *Transformables Collection*
2000
rubberized nylon mesh, Velcro, zippers
45 ¼ x 47 ¼ in. jacket
115 x 120 cm
66 ¹⁵/₁₆ x 74 ¹³/₁₆ in. kite
170 x 190 cm
Courtesy C.P. Company Transformables,
Ravarino, Italy

68–69. **Moreno Ferrari**
Sleeping Bag from *Transformables
Collection* 2000
rubberized nylon mesh
26 ¾ x 49 ⅝ in. jacket
68 x 126 cm
26 ¾ x 71 ⅝ in. sleeping bag
68 x 182 cm
Courtesy C.P. Company Transformables,
Ravarino, Italy

70–71. **Moreno Ferrari**
Tent from *Transformables Collection*
2000
rubberized nylon mesh, armature
59 ¹⁄₁₆ x 78 ¾ in. jacket
150 x 200 cm
78 ¾ x 74 ¹³⁄₁₆ in. tent
200 x 190 cm
Courtesy C.P. Company Transformables,
Ravarino, Italy

72. **Doug Garofalo**
Model of *Markow Residence* 2001
museum board, paint, basswood,
plywood
11 x 13 ½ x 27 ½ in.
27.94 x 34.29 x 69.85 cm
Courtesy Garofalo Architects, Chicago

73. **Markku Hedman**
Model of *Kesä-Kontti* (*Summer
Container*) 2001
wood, plywood, plexiglass
4 ¾ x 7 ¹⁄₁₆ x 5 ⅞ in. model
12 x 18 x 15 cm
Courtesy Markku Hedman, Helsinki

74. **Markku Hedman**
Model of *Etana* (*Snail*) 2003
wood, plywood, plexiglass, metal
sheeting
5 ⅛ x 11 ¹³⁄₁₆ x 14 ⁹⁄₁₆ in. model
13 x 30 x 37 cm
Courtesy Markku Hedman, Helsinki

75. **Koers, Zeinstra, van Gelderen**
Model of *Tumble House* 1998
birch three-ply wood
13 ¾ x 13 ¾ x 13 ¾ in.
35 x 35 x 35 cm
Courtesy Koers, Zeinstra, van Gelderen,
Amsterdam

*76. **Koers, Zeinstra, van Gelderen**
Tumble House 1998
plywood, hardwood, glass, stuffed
imitation leather
132 x 132 x 132 in.
335.28 x 335.28 x 335.28 cm
Courtesy Koers, Zeinstra, van Gelderen,
Amsterdam

77. **Koers, Zeinstra, van Gelderen**
Tumble House 1998
video transferred to DVD
Courtesy Koers, Zeinstra, van Gelderen,
Amsterdam

78. **LOT-EK**
Mobile Dwelling Unit (*MDU*) 2003
DVD
Courtesy LOT-EK (Giuseppe Lignano,
Ada Tolla), New York

*79. **LOT-EK**
   Mobile Dwelling Unit (*MDU*)   2003
   steel, plywood, plastic-laminated plywood, foam, rubber, steel framing, steel
   tracks, steel rollers, aluminum windows,
   fluorescent tubes, halogen light, bathroom and kitchen fixtures, appliances
   114 x 96 x 480 in. closed
   290 x 244 x 1,220 cm
   114 x 180 x 480 in. open
   290 x 457 x 1,220 cm
   Organized by the University Art
   Museum, University of California, Santa
   Barbara, and LOT-EK, New York

80. **MVRDV**
   Dutch Pavilion, Expo 2000   2000
   DVD
   Film by Hans Werleman
   Courtesy MVRDV (Winy Maas, Jacob
   van Rijs, Nathalie de Vries), Rotterdam

81. **MVRDV**
   Pig City   2001
   DVD
   Film by Wieland and Gouwens,
   Rotterdam
   Courtesy MVRDV (Winy Maas, Jacob
   van Rijs, Nathalie de Vries), Rotterdam

82. **Nucleo**
   Display model of *Terra: The Grass
   Arm-chair*   2000
   polypropylene, grass, soil, rocks
   47 ¼ x 47 ¼ x 23 ⅝ in.
   120 x 120 x 60 cm
   Courtesy Nucleo, Turin, Italy

83. **Nucleo**
   Terra: The Grass Arm-chair   2000
   cardboard
   47 ¼ x 47 ¼ x 23 ⅝ in.
   120 x 120 x 60 cm
   Courtesy Nucleo, Turin, Italy

84. **Marijn van der Poll**
   do hit   2001
   steel, lacquer, sledgehammer
   39 ⅜ x 29 ½ x 29 ½ in. steel chair
   100 x 75 x 75 cm
   4 ¾ x 5 ⅞ x 40 ½ in. sledgehammer
   13 x 15 x 103 cm
   Courtesy do create, Amsterdam

85. **R&Sie...**
   Habitat Furtif   1998
   DVD
   Courtesy R&Sie... (Stéphanie
   Lavaux, François Roche), Paris

86. **R&Sie...**
   Scrambled Flat   2001
   DVD
   Courtesy R&Sie... (Stéphanie
   Lavaux, François Roche), Paris

87. **Martín Ruiz de Azúa**
   Basic House   2000
   DVD
   Courtesy Martín Ruiz de Azúa,
   Barcelona

88. **Jennifer Siegal**
Model of *Portable House* 2001
Homasote board, bass wood,
plexiglass, brass
14 x 16 x 32 in. building model
36 x 41 x 81 cm
15 x 20 x 54 in. landscaped base
38 x 51 x 138 cm
Courtesy Office of Mobile Design,
Los Angeles

89. **Jennifer Siegal**
Portable House 2001
inkjet on paper
19 ⅞ x 39 ¹⁵⁄₁₆ in. each of 3
50.48 x 101.44 cm
Courtesy Office of Mobile Design,
Los Angeles

90. **Alejandro Stöberl**
Prefabricated Wooden House 2001
cedar, plexiglass
4 ¾ x 19 ¹¹⁄₁₆ x 11 ¹³⁄₁₆ in. overall
12 x 50 x 30 cm
Courtesy Alejandro Stöberl,
Buenos Aires

91. **su11 architecture+design**
Model of *Composite Housing* 2002
wood, cardboard, plastic, plexiglass
8 x 13 x 18 in.
20.32 x 45.72 x 33.02 cm
Courtesy su11 architecture+design
(Ferda Kolatan, Erich Schoenenberger),
New York

92. **su11 architecture+design**
*Process of Design, Fabrication, and
Installation* from *Composite Housing*
2002
interactive multimedia
Courtesy su11 architecture+design
(Ferda Kolatan, Erich Schoenenberger),
New York

93–94. **Frank Tjepkema and Peter van der Jagt**
do break 2001
porcelain, rubber, polyurethane
13 ⅜ x 5 ⅞ x 5 ⅞ in.
34 x 15 x 15 cm
Courtesy do create, Amsterdam

95. **Shigeru Uchida**
Gyo-an Paper Tea House 1995
wood, bamboo, spruce, paper
78 ¾ x 94 ½ x 94 ½ in.
200 x 240 x 240 cm
Collection The Conran Foundation,
London

96. **Shigeru Uchida**
Utensils for Gyo-an 2000
wood, aluminum, porcelain, bamboo,
mixed media
various sizes
Courtesy Shigeru Uchida, Tokyo

97. **Paolo Ulian**
Cabriolet/Occasional Table 2000/2002
wood
59 ¹⁄₁₆ x 35 ⁷⁄₁₆ x 13 ¾ in.
150 x 90 x 35 cm
Courtesy Paolo Ulian, Massa, Italy

98. **Paolo Ulian**
Greediness Meter 2002
dark chocolate
⅜ x 1 x 16 ⁹⁄₁₆ in.
.95 x 2.54 x 42.07 cm
Courtesy Paolo Ulian, Massa, Italy

99. **Paolo Ulian**
Greediness Meter 2002
white chocolate
⅜ x 1 x 16 ⁹⁄₁₆ in.
.95 x 2.54 x 42.07 cm
Courtesy Paolo Ulian, Massa, Italy

*100. **Marek Walczak, Michael McAllister, Jakub Segen, and Peter Kennard**
Dialog 2002–2003
resin, optically coated acrylic, glass, mirrors, memory gel, computers, projectors, cameras, printer, speakers
33 x 35 x 80 in.
83.82 x 88.9 x 203.2 cm
Commissioned by the Walker Art Center with support from the National Endowment for the Arts, 2002–2003

101. **Marcel Wanders**
Coryza from *Airborne Snotty Vases* 2001
polymide resin
5 ⅞ x 5 ⅞ x 5 ⅞ in.
15 x 15 x 15 cm
Collection John and Jean Geresi, Houston

102. **Marcel Wanders**
Influenza from *Airborne Snotty Vases* 2001
polymide resin
5 ⅞ x 5 ⅞ x 5 ⅞ in.
15 x 15 x 15 cm
Collection John and Jean Geresi, Houston

103. **Marcel Wanders**
Ozaena from *Airborne Snotty Vases* 2001
polymide resin
5 ⅞ x 5 ⅞ x 5 ⅞ in.
15 x 15 x 15 cm
Collection John and Jean Geresi, Houston

104. **Marcel Wanders**
Pollinosis from *Airborne Snotty Vases* 2001
polymide resin
5 ⅞ x 5 ⅞ x 5 ⅞ in.
15 x 15 x 15 cm
Collection John and Jean Geresi, Houston

105. **Marcel Wanders**
Sinusitis from *Airborne Snotty Vases* 2001
polymide resin
5 ⅞ x 5 ⅞ x 5 ⅞ in.
15 x 15 x 15 cm
Collection John and Jean Geresi, Houston

106. **Allan Wexler**
Gardening Sukkah 2000
wood structure, gardening implements, utensils
108 x 108 x 120 in.
274.32 x 274.32 x 304.8 cm
Courtesy Ronald Feldman Fine Arts, New York

107. **Rachel Whiteread**
Daybed 1999
beechwood frame, multidensity foams, wool upholstery
16 ¾ x 77 ½ x 33 ⅜ in.
42.55 x 196.85 x 84.77 cm
Courtesy A/D, New York

108. **www.fortunecookies.dk**
Felt 12x12 2001
DVD
Courtesy www.fortunecookies.dk,
Copenhagen

109. **www.fortunecookies.dk**
Felt 12x12 2001
felt, Velcro
23⅝ x 19¹¹⁄₁₆ in. jacket
60 x 50 cm
11¹³⁄₁₆ x 15¾ in. hat
40 x 30 cm
Courtesy www.fortunecookies.dk,
Copenhagen

110. **www.fortunecookies.dk**
Felt 12x12 2001
felt, Velcro, paperboard
5½ x 5½ x 1⁹⁄₁₆ in. box
14 x 14 x 3 cm
15¾ x 15¾ x 2¾ in. box
40 x 40 x 7 cm
Courtesy www.fortunecookies.dk,
Copenhagen

WALKER ART CENTER BOARD OF DIRECTORS, 2002–2003

Chairman
Stephen E. Watson

President
Roger L. Hale

Vice-Presidents
Arthur D. Collins, Jr.
Nadine McGuire
John G. Taft
C. Angus Wurtele

Secretary
Kathy Halbreich

Treasurer
Ann L. Bitter

Public Members
Elizabeth Andrus
Carol V. Bemis
Ann Birks
Ralph W. Burnet
Thomas M. Crosby, Jr.
Martha B. Dayton
Andrew S. Duff
M. Nazie Eftekhari

Jack Elliot
Jack W. Eugster
Matthew D. Fitzmaurice
Michael Francis
Martha Gabbert
L. Steven Goldstein
Andrew C. Grossman
Esperanza Guerrero-
  Anderson
Karen Heithoff
Martha H. Kaemmer
Sarah Kling
Anita H. Kunin
Sarah M. Lebedoff
Jeanne S. Levitt
Robert B. Mersky
J. Keith Moyer
Curtis Nelson
Mary Pappajohn
Michael A. Peel
Lawrence Perlman
Robyne Robinson
Stephen Shank
Michael T. Sweeney

Marjorie Weiser
Susan S. White
Frank Wilkinson

Walker Family Members
Ann Hatch
Kathleen S. Roeder
Adrian Walker
Brooks Walker, Jr.
Elaine B. Walker
Jean K. Walker
Lindsey Walker

Honorary Directors
H.B. Atwater, Jr.
Mrs. Julius E. Davis
Julia W. Dayton
Mrs. Malcolm A.
  McCannel
Harriet S. Spencer
Philip Von Blon
David M. Winton

Director Emeritus
Martin Friedman

343

First Edition © 2003 Walker Art Center
All rights reserved under pan-American copyright
conventions. No part of this book may be reproduced
or utilized in any form or by any means—electronic or
mechanical, including photocopying, recording, or by
any information storage-and-retrieval system—without
permission in writing from the Walker Art Center.
Inquiries should be addressed to: Publications Manager,
Walker Art Center, 725 Vineland Place, Minneapolis,
Minnesota 55403.

Available through D.A.P./Distributed Art Publishers,
155 Sixth Avenue, New York, NY 10013.

Every reasonable attempt has been made to identify owners
of copyright. Errors or omissions will be corrected in subse-
quent editions.

Designers Andrew Blauvelt and Alex DeArmond
Editors Pamela Johnson and Kathleen McLean
Publications Manager Lisa Middag
Curatorial Assistants Alisa Eimen and Sara Marion

Printed and bound in Germany by Cantz.

Library of Congress Cataloging-in-Publication Data
Strangely Familiar: Design and Everyday Life / Andrew
Blauvelt, curator.— 1st ed.
  p. cm.
Published on occasion of an exhibition held at Walker
Art Center, Minneapolis, Minn., June 8–Sept. 7, 2003,
Carnegie Museum of Art, Pittsburgh, Pa., Nov. 8,
2003–Feb. 15, 2004, and Musée de l'Hospice Comtesse,
Lille, France, Sept. 4–Nov. 28, 2004.
ISBN 0-935640-75-4 (flexible hardcover : alk. paper)
  1. Design—History—20th century—Exhibitions.
2. Design, Industrial—History—20th century—
Exhibitions. I. Blauvelt, Andrew, 1964– II. Walker Art
Center. III. Carnegie Museum of Art. IV. Musée de
l'Hospice Comtesse.
  NK1390.S77 2003
  745.2'09'04074776579—dc21

         2003007138

OIL CITY LIBRARY

DISCARD

0583 00169 2975

745.2
B613s
Blauvelt
Strangely familiar

Oil City Library
2 Central Ave.
Oil City, Pa.
Phone: 814-678-3072

Most library materials may be renewed by
phoning the above number.

A fine will be charged for each day a book is
overdue.

Mutilation of library books is punishable by
law with fine or imprisonment.

SEP 22 2004   GAYLORD F